MW00789229

Response to Intervention

Response to Intervention

Refining Instruction to Meet Student Needs

Timothy E. Morse

ROWMAN & LITTLEFIELD
Lanham • Boulder • New York • London

Published by Rowman & Littlefield
An imprint of The Rowman & Littlefield Publishing Group, Inc.
4501 Forbes Boulevard, Suite 200, Lanham, Maryland 20706
www.rowman.com

6 Tinworth Street, London SE11 5AL

Copyright © 2020 by Timothy E. Morse

All rights reserved. No part of this book may be reproduced in any form or by any electronic or mechanical means, including information storage and retrieval systems, without written permission from the publisher, except by a reviewer who may quote passages in a review.

British Library Cataloguing in Publication Information Available

Library of Congress Control Number: 2019953372

ISBN 978-1-4758-4407-8 (cloth : alk. paper)
ISBN 978-1-4758-4408-5 (pbk. : alk. paper)
ISBN 978-1-4758-4409-2 (electronic)

∞ ™ The paper used in this publication meets the minimum requirements of American National Standard for Information Sciences Permanence of Paper for Printed Library Materials, ANSI/NISO Z39.48-1992.

To George and Phyllis Morse and
Billy Ray and Loretta Smith.
Thanks for everything.

Contents

Preface

My work as a special educator began forty years ago when I enrolled in my undergraduate program. During this time, I have completed several degree granting programs and accumulated a wealth of professional experiences that have enabled me to see, from numerous vantage points, how the field of education operates. These programs and experiences include the following:

1. Bachelor's, master's, and doctorate degrees in special education. These degrees pertain to students with mild disabilities, moderate to significant disabilities, special education administration, assistive technology applications in special education, and instructional design.
2. Various positions as a special education teacher, grades P-12, in resource and self-contained classrooms. I have also provided support to students with disabilities in general education classrooms.
3. Employment as an assistant director of special education in school district with 20,000 students.
4. Experiences as both an assistant and associate professor of special education.
5. A seven year long stint as the director of training/positive behavior support specialist for an Autism Demonstration School that I developed and founded.

As a result of all of these activities I have learned that what I enjoy doing the most is working with aspiring or new teachers in ways that enable them to develop solid foundational teaching skills while also understanding how what they do "in the trenches" fits into a school's master plan. For a school to be able to meet the needs of each student, every teacher must be successful in her work, and the work of every teacher must interconnect properly with all of the other educators' work.

My interest in working with teachers to enable them to develop basic, effective teaching skills is based on a personal belief and two interrelated professional experiences. My personal belief is that the majority of our students could demonstrate markedly higher levels of academic achievement and rates of learning if every teacher demonstrated fundamentally sound teaching practices daily.

These practices primarily consist of what are known as universal effective teaching practices combined with effective subject matter practices. This belief resulted from two interrelated professional experiences that I share next.

In my roles as a university professor and special education administrator, I visited and conducted formal observations in numerous classrooms. On many more occasions than I ever cared or hoped to see, I would witness ongoing activities in general education classrooms that were neither well-organized nor well-defined.

In general, my visit would consist of me spending the first ten minutes trying to figure out the learning objective(s) that was the focus of the teacher's instruction. By the time I figured it out I was both exhausted from the effort and frustrated that the teacher had not taken it upon herself to make her intentions clearly known.

I then did my best to follow the rest of the lesson. While in most instances matters did improve somewhat, often and not surprisingly in many instances the teacher failed to demonstrate more effective, evidence-based instructional strategies during the middle and end of the lesson than she did at the beginning.

One outcome of these experiences was asking myself how a typical student or a student with a disability was able to profit from these lessons when I, with my advanced degrees and years of experience as both a teacher and an administrator, was not able to readily discern what a student was expected to learn from the lesson.

Now contrast the previous experiences with an experience I had as a special education support teacher in a ninth grade Algebra 1 class.

The general education teacher had taught junior high math for several years and was working for the first time as a high school math teacher. Interestingly, she was working toward her licensure as an Algebra 1 teacher.

As was the case when she taught junior high math, her Algebra 1 students' end of course standardized test scores were among the highest in both the school district and the state. Despite not being a subject matter expert, she was able to get her students to perform as well as they did because, daily, she exhibited strong, fundamental teaching practices, which included the following:

1. At the outset of each lesson she clearly stated, both orally and in writing, the day's learning objective(s).
2. She designed and managed an environmental arrangement that enabled each student to attend to her instruction and perform related tasks (e.g., sharpen pencils, turn in assignments) so as not to disrupt the lesson.
3. Throughout each lesson she focused exclusively on curriculum content and employed techniques such as requiring active student responding to comprehension check questions, which resulted in students also focusing exclusively on this content.
4. She taught from "bell to bell," resulting in various types of effective time management, including allocated, engaged, and academic learning time.
5. Her assessments were aligned with her curriculum. Further, she used the data she obtained from these assessments to inform her instruction.
6. She presented content in appropriate chunks, used key vocabulary, and balanced three types of instruction: teacher-led, guided practice, and independent practice.

Hence, I have written this book because I believe that the topic—the response-to-intervention (RTI) framework—afforded me the opportunity to teach beginning teachers about sound, fundamental teaching practices while also informing them how their work implementing these practices interconnects with various types of effective instruction that is presented throughout a school so that the needs of each student are met. These needs are met when each student receives the effective, individualized instruction that is available to them as a result of how the framework is designed and operated.

As I state from the outset of the book, while there are many features to a response-to-intervention framework, two stand out as solid reasons why school personnel should be familiar with its basic structure. One reason is that it provides a sound protocol to account for the performance of every student. A second reason is that it provides a structure that is useful for figuring out how to refine instruction so that it is individualized to meet each student's needs.

By reading this book you will learn that an important aspect of the framework is its central focus on the provision of high-quality instruction in every general education classroom. I believe that this focus, and the framework's continual referencing to the general education classroom as other components of the framework are explained, allows for an authentic and deep understanding of the multi-faceted nature of public-school education. This includes seeing special education as a value-added, supplemental service rather than a separate, wholly detached program.

Consequently, if you develop a fundamental understanding of this framework you will be able to understand what a school that is using it is attempting to accomplish on behalf of every student, and both how and why they are going about doing so.

Based on everything I laid out above, I decided to write this book. I believe it contains important, basic information that teachers need to know in order to be effective in their own right. Additionally, the book explains how the varied services that are provided throughout a response-to-intervention framework interconnect such that every student attending school will be provided effective, individualized instruction.

Acknowledgments

Like many worthwhile undertakings, the completion of this endeavor resulted from the contributions of a group of competent colleagues. I need to thank Sarah Wicks for her diligent efforts ensuring that the final manuscript adhered to the publisher's guidelines. Additionally, thanks go to Dr. Beverly Morse, Dr. Sandi McLaughlin, Marie Wicks, and Michelle Andrews for reviewing the book for clarity and applicability.

Finally, I am grateful for the support that was extended from the extremely patient staff at Rowman & Littlefield. They kept this project going while, at various times, I had to attend to other matters that resulted in a delay of the finished product.

Introduction

While there are many features of a response-to-intervention framework, two stand out as solid reasons why school personnel should be familiar with its basic structure. One reason is that it provides a sound protocol to account for the performance of every student. A second reason is that it provides a structure that is useful for figuring out how to refine instruction so that it is individualized to meet each student's needs.

However, this refinement is only possible when the elements that comprise the framework are clearly defined. When they are, school personnel can identify the aspects of instruction that need to be changed so that effective instruction is presented to a student who, heretofore, has not attained targeted learning outcomes.

While this book can be useful to both beginning and experienced teachers as well as other professionals who provide direct and indirect services to students, it has been written first and foremost with preservice teachers in mind. It should prove to be useful to these teachers by enabling them to identify the following:

1. The knowledge and skills they need to acquire in their preparation program
2. The questions they need to be prepared to ask and answer during a job interview
3. The work they need to perform in the role they will fill in a school that uses a response-to-intervention framework

Focus of the book

When I consider my stance with respect to the appropriateness of an RTI framework I think of my experiences as an assistant special education director in a school district with nearly 20,000 students. Without fail, at the end of each school year I would be told by several teachers who worked in different schools and had used different reading programs that the school district needed to abandon the commercial reading program that the teacher had been using because "it didn't work." After examining the programs and noting that each was evidence-based and covered the content that needed to be taught—albeit by employing somewhat different lessons—I concluded that what really needed to happen was for the teachers to settle upon one program, use it as it was designed to the best of their ability, and then brainstorm with colleagues about ways they could make it more effective. Specifically, they needed to supplement the program with instruction that was calculated to be effective in ways that the commercial program had not been. This calculation needed to be based on student performance data and analyses of the teachers' instruction.

I feel that same way about the response-to-intervention framework that is the focus of this book as I did about the commercial reading programs. A response-to-intervention framework is comprised of evidence-based elements that will lead to the provision of effective instruction. Yet, it will need to be refined for a number of reasons, including the unique characteristics of each school in which it is employed and the students' achievement data. Thus, I see it as having staying power over the long haul as opposed to being a passing fad so long as educators dedicate themselves to performing the painstaking work that is involved with each aspect of the protocol. Simply stated, the phrase "quality takes time" applies.

As I explain in chapter 1, while various terms are in use to refer to the type of multi-tier model that a response-to-intervention framework is, I have settled upon the term response-to-intervention because it captures the essence of teaching, which is to continue to present instruction to students based on how they responded to the instruction that was presented beforehand. Hence, this book is a discussion about the issues that must be addressed to enable a school to realize its goal of presenting effective, appropriate instruction to every student rather than a step-by-step explanation of how to implement this particular way of designing a school's approach to instructional programming. In my opinion the essential question that needs to be asked to, and answered by, those who want to discount a response-to-intervention framework is, "If not RTI, then what?"

Organization of the book

The seven chapters that comprise the handbook address three broad topics: the structure of a response-to-intervention framework, the fundamental premises and components of the framework, and practical considerations pertaining to its implementation.

Chapter 1 presents an overview of the framework. The framework is defined and its two basic components—assessment and tiered intervention services—are described. As you will learn, the framework's tiered intervention services essentially function as a classification system for matching students to the type of instructional services they need. While RTI frameworks can differ in terms of the number of intervention tiers, a three-tier framework is described in this handbook. Chapter 1 also presents some historical background information that pertains to the origination of the response-to-intervention framework and a list of reasons why you should learn about it.

Chapters 2 and 3 focus on Tier 1 services and the framework's emphasis that these services consist of high quality, scientifically based instruction that is to be provided to all students in the general education classroom. Chapter 2 discusses several ways that high quality instruction could be conceptualized, and then operationally defines the term such that one can readily identify if it is being provided or, if not, how a teacher's design and operation of her classroom can be reconfigured so that this type of instruction is presented.

Chapter 3 explains the meaning of scientifically based instruction. First, the chapter describes how a scientific experiment is conducted and experimental research designs are used to identify instructional strategies that are effective in terms of enabling students to attain targeted learning outcomes. Second, the process that is followed to conduct what is known as an evidence-based review to identify effective instructional strategies that are supported by multiple research studies is explained. These instructional strategies are called evidence-based practices.

The Tier 2 services that are provided in the framework are the subject of chapter 4. As is noted in this chapter and elsewhere in the book, these services are characterized by the use of small group arrangements and the provision of more intense intervention than was provided in Tier 1. Hence, throughout chapter 4's discussion of Tier 2 services, comparisons are made between these services and the Tier 1 services that function as the foundation, or baseline, for intervention services in the framework.

General features of Tier 2 services as well as the concept of intensive intervention are presented near the outset of the chapter. This presentation is followed by an explanation of small group instruction and how intensive intervention can be configured to meet the needs of students who, throughout their school careers, have consistently exhibited challenges mastering grade-level, targeted learning outcomes but have not been determined to be eligible to receive special education services.

Chapter 5 focuses on special education and its relationship to the other components in a response-to-intervention framework. Special education comprises Tier 3 of the RTI framework that is described in this book.

As is noted in chapter 1, an assessment component is one of the two primary components of the framework. Accordingly, in chapter 6 basic information about school-based assessment that is pertinent to your understanding of a response-to-intervention framework is discussed.

A conscious decision was made to address the role of instruction in a response-to-intervention framework at the outset of this book while subsequently putting the spotlight on assessment. This approach differs from that of a number of other authors who have written about the framework. At the beginning of their manuscripts they have addressed the topic of assessment if, for no other reason, then the fact that screening is to be conducted from the outset of the implementation of the framework so as to be able to appropriately place each student within whatever tiers have been established in the framework that is being described.

Since this activity is considered to be a bit more of a concern to the school administrators who will oversee the implementation of a response-to-intervention framework, and this book is geared toward teachers, the decision was made to address assessment issues throughout the first part of the book whenever doing so was deemed to be relevant. Then, in the latter part of the book this extremely relevant topic would be addressed in a manner consistent with the book's focus on its target audience: beginning teachers.

The final chapter of the book, chapter 7, presents a number of considerations that are central to the design and operation of an RTI framework. In particular, the chapter seeks to highlight issues of practical significance that will enhance your understanding of a protocol that has been characterized as having the potential to serve as the basis for true school reform in the United States.

Chapter One

RTI From a Teacher's Perspective

OVERVIEW

In this chapter you will learn about a protocol, called Response-to-Intervention (RTI) framework, that schools can follow to account for the performance of every student as well as systematically refine their instruction so that it is individualized to meet each student's needs. Key points from the chapter include the following:

A response-to-intervention framework refers to a systematic process that involves the use of a student's performance data to match him with the types of services that will increase the probability that he will attain targeted learning outcomes.

This framework is composed of two essential components: an assessment component and a tiered intervention component.

The assessment component consists of screeners that are designed to identify students who are at-risk for attaining targeted learning outcomes. Additionally, it consists of progress monitoring assessments that identify the level at which a student is performing, as well as the rate at which the student learns new material.

The framework's tiered intervention component is a classification system that is used to match students to the intervention services they require to address their learning needs.

RTI frameworks originated from a need to (a) identify—as accurately as possible—students with specific learning disabilities and (b) provide instruction beyond what is available in a general education classroom to students who perform similarly to students with specific learning disabilities in terms of academic achievement but have not been determined to be eligible to receive special education services.

There are a number of frameworks that are similar to a response-to-intervention framework in terms of design and implementation. In this book, the term "RTI" framework is used exclusively because it captures the essence of all the frameworks that school personnel use to educate students based on how they respond to the provided interventions.

There are a number of reasons why beginning teachers need to know about a response-to-intervention framework, including the fact that more than 70 percent of school districts across the country incorporate an RTI framework in at least some classrooms. It has been referred to as having the potential to serve as the basis for true school reform in the United States.

RESPONSE-TO-INTERVENTION: ANOTHER SCHOOL REFORM

Some veteran educators probably cannot remember a time during their career when the term "school reform" was absent during a discussion concerning how our nation's schools should function. Given one definition for the word "reform," which is to improve upon the way that something is currently being done, it is understandable why the term school reform always has been, and probably will be, a part of such discussions.

Accordingly, the focus of this book is an ongoing, multi-component school reform effort and the work that teachers are to perform with respect to it. This version of school reform has evolved over time and has been identified by various names, including Response-to-Intervention (RTI), School-wide Positive Behavior Interventions and Supports (SWPBIS), and Multitier Systems of Support (MTSS). Throughout most of this book, the term "RTI framework" will be used in place of all the aforementioned names. Below the reasoning for this arrangement, as well as a brief discussion about the evolution of this ongoing multi-component school reform effort, is presented.

What is Response-to-Intervention?

This framework is a systematic process that consists of using student performance data to match students with the types of services that increase the probability that they will attain expected learning outcomes (i.e., targeted academic and school social behaviors). These services are explained in terms of tiers, with the first tier consisting of the instruction that is provided to every student in the general education classroom. Subsequent tiers consist of services provided to progressively smaller groups of students who are performing at a much lower level and learning at a much slower rate than their peers. These services become more individualized with respect to the content that is taught and the instructional strategies that are used.

Even though the response-to-intervention framework has been around for nearly two decades, much remains to be learned about its use and effectiveness. A recent investigation of the use of an academic-focused Response-to-Intervention framework in 146 schools called into question whether it was being implemented as designed and its overall effectiveness in terms of student achievement. In fact, some who critiqued the investigation remarked that we are still awaiting a valid, national study of RTI's effectiveness. [1]

The current debate, pertaining to whether RTI is being implemented as designed and, as a result, is having a positive result on students' attainments of expected learning outcomes, is not surprising when considered with respect to other studies of comprehensive school reforms. Longitudinal studies of some of these reforms revealed that fewer than 50 percent of teachers received training on the chosen practice, fewer than 10 percent of the schools used the reforms as intended, and most students did not benefit. [2]

COMPONENTS OF AN RTI FRAMEWORK

The response-to-intervention framework is composed of two essential components: an assessment component and a tiered intervention component. It is important to note that the number of tiers within this type of framework can vary, and this circumstance is another example of how it is conceptual in nature. In this book, a three-tier framework serves as the basis for the information that is presented.

Assessment Component

The assessment component consists of (a) screening and (b) ongoing progress monitoring. A screener is an assessment instrument that is used for a predetermined purpose to sort out a relatively small number of students from a much larger group. For example, at the very beginning of the school year a first-grade teacher would be interested in knowing which students in her class demonstrated noteworthy academic deficits, relative to their peers, that have been shown to be related to one's subsequent acquisition of proficient reading skills. This small number of students would be said to be at risk for becoming a proficient reader unless some type of intervention that was systematically designed to remediate their deficit was employed.

Progress monitoring assessments provide data about the rate at which a student is attaining the expected learning outcomes as well as the total number of outcomes the student has attained. The measure of the total number of outcomes attained is referred to as a student's level of learning and is related to what is referred to as the scope of a school's curriculum. Issues that pertain to the assessment component of a response-to-intervention framework are discussed in more detail in chapter 6.

Tiered Intervention Component

At its core, a response-to-intervention framework's tiered intervention component is a classification system. Students are classified according to which tier they have been placed in for the purpose of getting the intervention services they need to address their learning needs. Thus, the tiered intervention component involves a process in which data obtained from the model's assessment component is evaluated so that a student can be matched with the intervention services that are provided in one of the model's different tiers.

The number of tiers can differ from one school to another. In this book, a three-tier model is explained. However, a school that has the necessary resources that enable them to more precisely refine the intervention services that are provided from tier to tier may use a protocol that consists of five tiers of intervention services rather than three. An RTI framework's flexibility in this regard is the primary reason why the focus of this book is the broad features and principles that are characteristic of any iteration of the framework, rather than a step-by-step, cookbook approach to the design and implementation of the framework (i.e., meaning an approach in which a sequential list of steps must be completed for the one, true response-to-intervention framework to be implemented).

Tier 1 is the category that consists of students who are mastering grade-level standards for academic content and appropriate social behaviors while receiving instruction exclusively in the general education classroom.

Tier 2 is the category that consists of students who, despite being instructed in the general education classroom, have not mastered grade-level academic content or school social behaviors (i.e., students who are said to be low achieving or at-risk). Thus, they need to receive additional interventions that are intended to remediate their deficits.

Finally, Tier 3 is the category that consists of students who have been determined to be eligible to receive special education services. These students' services will be provided in accordance with an individualized education plan (IEP).

The intervention services that are provided in each tier are differentiated by features such as the content being taught, the process that is used to identify this content, the conditions that are in place when instruction is presented, and how often assessment data are collected and analyzed. Tier 2 and Tier 3 services are said to differ from Tier 1 services with respect to the nature and intensity of the instruction that is presented. In general, tier services differ with respect to (a) group size and (b) the provision of more explicit, intense instruction.[3]

Tier 1: High-Quality, Scientifically Based Instruction in the General Education Classroom

The foundation for the implementation of an RTI framework is the instruction that is presented in general education classrooms. A fundamental premise of the framework is that Tier 1 intervention services will consist of high quality, scientifically-based instruction that will enable at least 75–80 percent of the students to attain grade-level academic skill and social behavior standards. This instruction comprises Tier 1 of the framework and, therefore, means that the general education classroom serves as the reference point for all subsequent RTI activities.

Additionally, in order to enhance your understanding of how intervention services differ between tiers, in this book's discussion of the framework it is presumed that large group arrangements (i.e., pupil: teacher ratios of 20–30+:1) predominate in these classrooms. That is to say, small group arrangements, 1:1 arrangements, peer-to-peer instruction, and technology-based instruction may be used at times in these classrooms, both as an additional means of instruction for all students as well as a way to present remedial instruction to low achieving students. However, since small group arrangements are a distinguishing feature of both Tier 2 and Tier 3 intervention services, in this book they will be juxtaposed with the large group arrangements that predominate in Tier 1.

Tier 2: Small Group Instruction with Increased Intensity

In the framework Tier 2 intervention services will be provided to an estimated 20–25 percent students who do not attain grade-level content standards after receiving Tier 1 intervention services. Tier 1 instruction in the general education classroom would continue to be provided to these students, but this instruction would be supplemented with what the framework refers to as more intense instruction that would be provided in a small group arrangement.

Tier 2 intervention services are intended to remediate a student's academic skill or social behavior deficits. When this remediation occurs (i.e., the student is now performing at grade level), the student would be placed back in Tier 1 where, hopefully, he would forevermore maintain his achievement of grade-level standards.

Students who demonstrate adequate progress after receiving Tier 2 intervention services, but do not remediate their deficits (i.e., have not achieved grade-level standards), will continue to receive these supplemental services. Students who demonstrate minimal or no progress after receiving Tier 2 intervention services will be provided Tier 3 services. Tier 3 services will be provided to these students after they have been referred for an initial evaluation that results in a determination that they are eligible to receive special education services. Tier 2 services are discussed in chapter 4.

Tier 3: Special Education Services

Tier 3 is the category that consists of students who have been determined to be eligible to receive special education services and, as a result, have individualized education plans (IEPs) that document these services. According to the framework, 5–10 percent of students will receive these services. Tier 3 services are discussed in chapter 5.

PRINCIPLES OF AN RTI FRAMEWORK

The principles that underlie this framework are the central elements that distinguish the framework from other approaches to school reform. Advocates for the framework assert that the way that its elements work in a comprehensive, coordinated fashion is noteworthy. As was just noted, the interconnectedness of this framework includes an assessment component comprised of screening and ongoing progress monitoring, as well as an intervention services component that includes the presentation of high-quality instruction in the general education classrooms to all students. Additionally, intensive, remedial interventions are provided in small group arrangements to a relatively small percentage of students who did not attain grade-level academic and behavior standards after receiving only high-quality instruction in the general education classroom.

Others[4] posited that there are five clearly defined principles that underlie any response-to-intervention framework and four features that evolve from these principles. Both the principles and features are discussed below.

Response-to-Intervention's Five Principles

1. It is a proactive and preventative approach to education. Beginning with its use of screening to identify students who may be at risk for failure, an RTI framework is designed to provide additional services to students who need them as an effort to ensure the students' success. This is characterized as a proactive approach because additional services are provided before a school waits to see if the student does, in fact, fail while only being provided large group instruction in the general education classroom.

   It is a preventative approach because it not only reduces the chances that a student will fail but also reduces the chances that a student will erroneously be identified as having a disability that is presumed to be the basis for his substandard academic achievement or inadequate displays of appropriate school social behaviors when, in fact, this circumstance is the result of inappropriate instruction.

This principle highlights how the framework addresses some of the provisions in our nation's federal special education law that pertain to the identification of students with disabilities, particularly those with a specific learning disability. One provision is an exclusionary criterion which means that, before a student can be identified as meeting the eligibility criteria for a specific learning disability, the multidisciplinary evaluation and eligibility determination team must exclude the fact that the reason for the student's academic or school social behavior deficits is his lack of exposure to appropriate instruction.

2. It ensures an instructional match between a student's skills, curriculum, and instruction. An RTI framework's tiered intervention services are designed to place students in a context in which the core curriculum content they need to learn is taught under instructional conditions that are best suited to the student's needs.

3. Both a problem-solving orientation and data-based decision making are used. Ongoing progress monitoring provides schools with data they can analyze to make informed decisions such as (a) how to adjust the instruction that is being presented in the different tiers so that it is effective, (b) which students to place in these tiers, and (c) whether a student needs to be evaluated to determine his eligibility for the receipt of special education services.

4. The use of effective practices is key. Central to the framework is the provision of what is referred to as high-quality, scientifically-based instruction in the general education classroom. Chapter 2 addresses what is meant by high-quality instruction while chapter 3 explains scientifically-based instruction.

5. It is a systems-level approach. While the framework focuses on the intervention services that are provided to each student, this focus is part of the framework's overarching comprehensive, coordinated approach that is to be employed by an entire school district or school. When the framework is employed by an entire school district, vertical integration, which refers to the coordination of efforts across elementary, middle, and high schools, must be addressed. Likewise, when the model is employed in a school, both vertical integration across grade levels and horizontal integration across classrooms within a grade level must be addressed.

Response-to-Intervention's Four Features

The four features of the framework that evolve from these principles are as follows:

1. The use of multiple tiers. These refer to the framework's tiers of differentiated intervention services. As was noted previously, the tiers essentially constitute a classification system for the placement of students in accordance with the content they need to learn and the services they need to be provided to learn the content.
2. The use of an assessment system. A response-to-intervention framework calls for the use of an assessment system that is comprised of two basic components: a universal screener and progress monitoring.
3. Protocols that guide the implementation of the framework. These protocols will be site-specific and, therefore, highly individualized. They will address an expansive range of topics, such as (a) how and when screening will be conducted; (b) what constitutes high-quality content area instruction, such as beginning reading instruction as well as instruction to develop a student's social competence; and, (c) the criteria for placing students in each tier.
4. Presenting evidence-based instruction. Essentially, evidence-based instruction refers to the use of objective data as the primary basis for making instructional decisions. In the framework, the starting point for the use of evidence-based instruction is the high-quality instruction that is to be scientifically-based and is presented in the general education classroom. Additionally, while screening and ongoing progress monitoring data are collected and analyzed for the reasons described previously, these data also lead to the provision of another type of evidence-based instruction.

THE RTI FRAMEWORK AND A SCHOOL'S WORK SCOPE

The response-to-intervention framework is a protocol that school personnel can use to address their need to account for the performance of every student in the general education, or core curriculum. It is a conceptual framework that provides for a process that school personnel can follow to ensure that they are implementing interventions such as scientifically-based instruction and data-based program modifications, which will result in the adequate progress of every student in the general education curriculum.[5]

Among other things this description of the framework highlights the fact that there is not a single way to define, construct, and implement it. Hence, the approach taken in this book's explanation of the framework is like that taken by others[6] who, rather than identifying and discussing specific steps that need to be completed to ensure that *the* RTI framework is implemented properly, discussed general principles and features that characterize a true response-to-intervention framework.

The RTI framework received noteworthy attention when in 2004 the law, that directs the provision of special education services by America's schools—the Individuals with Disabilities Education Improvement Act (IDEA)[7]—referenced the use of a response-to-intervention approach to identify children with specific learning disabilities. By extension this meant that the embodiment of this approach in the framework could be used to direct a school-wide process for accounting for the performance of every student in the general education curriculum: those who are functioning at or above grade level, those who are not meeting grade level standards and could be considered at risk for school failure, and those who qualify for the receipt of special education services. This also meant that the framework could be used to systematically address the scope of the work that school personnel must perform, which includes:

1. Providing instruction in the general education classroom that addresses core curriculum standards and involves the use of scientifically-based interventions
2. Conducting valid, reliable assessments that are aligned with core curriculum standards
3. Evaluating the assessment data to determine which students are demonstrating adequate progress in the general education curriculum versus those who are not and, therefore, need to be provided some type of remedial instruction
4. Providing remedial instruction systematically to low achieving, at-risk students with the intent to rectify deficits in their level of achievement and rate of progress
5. Performing child find activities to identify children with disabilities who are eligible for the receipt of special education services
6. Providing special education services

The fact that any school's staff can develop and then use the framework in a way that meets their unique needs to perform their entire work scope while accounting for each student's performance in the general education curriculum is one impetus for writing this book. Accordingly, the range of topics addressed in the book includes the conceptual basis for the framework, information regarding how to perform some of its intervention services and practical considerations regarding its use.

The intent of this effort is to enable you to determine how the framework can be used, and how you can work in it to address relevant issues in this era of school accountability. Conversely, the hope is that you do not find yourself tolerating the existence of a response-to-intervention framework as another passing fad in the field of education that falls under the heading of school reform.

WHY RESPONSE-TO-INTERVENTION?
WHERE DID IT COME FROM?

Knowing the circumstances that led to the creation of this framework may further your understanding of its design and operation. The below five items that have contributed, to varying degrees, to the development and use of this framework are identified and discussed.

Origin of the RTI Framework: Accurate Identification of Students with Specific Learning Disabilities

The origin of the response-to-intervention framework has been directly attributed to a concerted effort to create a way to more accurately identify students with a specific learning disability. A particular concern was how these students were being distinguished from the population of low achieving, but non-disabled, students in a school. This matter is discussed in more detail below. For now, the focus is on the fact that since nearly half of all students who are determined to be eligible to receive special education services are identified as such after meeting the criteria for the category of specific learning disability. Concerns about the accurate identification of these students warrant attention.

Theoretical Basis for a Specific Learning Disability

A student with a specific learning disability is presumed to possess average to above average intelligence but demonstrate academic achievement scores that are much lower than would be expected given the individual's base level of intelligence. The student's academic performance is said to be discrepant with his intelligence, and the degree or extent of this discrepancy (which is supposed to be severe or significant, although the way it is quantified varies across states) is the basis upon which a diagnosis of a specific learning disability is made.

The reason for this discrepancy is presumed to result from differences in one's basic psychological processes (e.g., short-term visual and auditory memory skills). Regardless of the validity of this presumption, there is concern that the IQ-achievement discrepancy approach fails to distinguish a qualitatively different and more deserving subgroup of students from a much larger group of low achieving students who are nondisabled.[8, 9, 10, 11, 12, 13, 14, 15, 16]

Addressing the Exclusionary Criterion Within an RTI Framework

To increase confidence, or enhance the validity, in the underlying cause and theoretical basis for a specific learning disability, it is necessary to exclude a very plausible reason why a student would demonstrate poor academic achievement despite possessing average to above-average intelligence: the student had not been provided appropriate formal instruction. Thus, the relevance of ensuring that high-quality instruction is being, or has been, presented to a student in the general education classroom is important not only for understanding and implementing a response-to-intervention framework with fidelity, but also because of its centrality to the logic behind the determination of a specific learning disability that will allow a child to be eligible to receive special education services.

The basis for this logic is as follows: the learning challenges that a child is manifesting are the result of a disabling condition rather than an external factor which, if addressed properly, would enable the student to demonstrate that he can master the academic content he is being taught. This reasoning explains, in part, why guidelines are established for how long a student must be presented formal instruction before the process of officially evaluating the student for the presence of a disability may be initiated.

The term *dysteachia* has been used to refer to instances where a child's demonstrated lack of progress has been the result of exposure to poor instruction rather than an inherent disability. When this is the case, it is both necessary and ethical to correct instructional deficiencies rather than attribute a child's low performance to child-centered deficits such as a specific learning disability.

The circumstance described above explains, in part, why the framework is tied directly to the special education eligibility determination process. Yet, this circumstance also highlights how the framework is a mechanism for determining the conditions that need to be put in place in order for each student to be afforded a high probability of demonstrating mastery of the general education curriculum—whatever the extent of that mastery will turn out to be.

The framework recognizes that a certain percentage of students will need to be provided interventions in addition to, and somewhat different from, those that are provided in a general education classroom. It is estimated that 20–30 percent of all students will need to be provided Tier 2 services and 5–10 percent Tier 3 services.

The key point is that the focus is on service provision throughout a RTI framework, and for every student. In other words, while the framework provides a sound mechanism for identifying students who are eligible to receive special education services, this should not be how the use of the framework is thought about by educators. Rather, the framework should be thought of as a mechanism for finding a way to provide effective instruction that enables every student to master the content in the core curriculum. This perspective likely explains why the framework has been adopted as a general education practice after having originated as a special education initiative.

Desire for Cost-Efficient Schools

The issue of the cost of special education services is closely linked to the accurate identification of students who are eligible to receive these services. The desire to reduce the cost of special education services, in and of itself, has not been cited as a driving force behind the creation and use of the framework. Rather, these costs have been discussed within the context of figuring out ways that schools can use the resources that are available to them to meet the needs of every student who is demonstrating difficulty mastering grade level content.

For instance, there have been claims that the costs of special education have been borne, to some degree, by low achieving students who were not performing demonstrably different from some of the students who were being provided special education services. These low achieving students received either limited, or no, services beyond what was provided to them in the general education classroom. This circumstance is why these students have been depicted as being "students who fell into an instructional crack," meaning the gap that exists between instruction in the general education classroom and the point at which special education services are provided.

Some research indicates that, relative to the cost of general education instruction, special education services are two to three times more expensive. This cost ratio in and of itself is worthy of examination given the limited funds available to public schools and, therefore, the need to manage them in a way that results in the greatest efficiencies possible (i.e., the greatest productivity in terms of the amount of student achievement relative to the services provided to produce this achievement).[17] It becomes an even greater concern when one considers the multiplier effect that is realized each time a student is determined to be eligible to receive special education services when he should not have been.

The RTI framework has been championed as a way to ensure that students with disabilities and their low achieving, nondisabled peers who are functioning similarly receive appropriate instructional services because both the mechanism and the money for providing them is available via the framework.

Emergence of Scientifically-based, Effective Early Reading Instruction

Closely related to the manner, in which students with a specific learning disability, are identified is the primary reason why they are identified: failure to achieve grade level reading standards. Research about (a) how to identify students who are at risk for reading failure; (b) the content they need to be taught in order to become a proficient, independent reader; and, (c) the establishment of effective, evidence based practices for teaching beginning reading instruction also contributed to the creation of the framework since knowing how to present this effective, evidence-based instruction contributes to the accurate identification of students with a specific learning disability.

Era of School Accountability

In the not too distant past, schools were evaluated on measures that pertained to their resources. For instance, a school whose teachers had advanced degrees, was equipped with a library and science lab, and had an adequate ratio of square footage per student was deemed to be of better quality than a school that did not have these resources.

This way of evaluating schools certainly has changed as schools presently are evaluated based upon measures that pertain to their students' performances, particularly measures of their academic achievement even though some measures of school social behavior (e.g., suspension rates) are more frequently being included in these evaluations. Presently, an RTI framework has been adopted by many schools to address this circumstance.

With respect to providing effective instruction that results in improvements in students' academic achievement, until the mid-1970s public school personnel were not required to educate every child, let alone account for their progress in the general education curriculum. At that time, some children with disabilities were excluded from attending public schools altogether. It was not until 1975, when the 94th Congress of the United States passed what is now known as the Individuals with Disabilities Education Act (IDEA),[18] that the guarantee of a free and appropriate public-school education for every child was secured.

The IDEIA stipulated that every child with a disability, irrespective of the significance of its impact on a child's functioning, was entitled to a free and appropriate public-school education. Furthermore, the legislation required school personnel to document what they would teach a child with a disability, the special education services they would provide, and any evidence that indicated the child had benefitted from his school program. With this arrangement in place, the stage was finally set for holding the nation's public schools accountable for the educational attainment of every student.

More recent legislation—both the No Child Left Behind Act[19] and its successor, the Every Student Succeeds Act[20]—has functioned in a manner similar to the IDEIA with respect to ensuring that every student is afforded an appropriate, meaningful education. One matter that is addressed in both pieces of legislation and is particularly relevant to this book's focus is the accountability provisions that pertain to students' academic progress in the general education curriculum and related outcomes, such as high school graduation rates.

In terms of school social behavior, measures that relate to students being in school so that they can profit from the academic instruction that is presented are evaluated. One example would be a school's suspension rate. Perhaps most noteworthy is the way in which the legislation requires schools to disaggregate their accountability data such that there is a transparent accounting of each student's performance.

The term *school accountability* has been coined to refer to the larger phenomenon, which can be described as an evolving movement in the field of education to require schools to collect and report data pertaining to students' progress in the general education curriculum. In turn, these data serve various functions, including validating both the appropriateness and effectiveness of the educational services that schools provide, and allowing for a system of grading schools in a way that enables them to be compared.

The circumstance described above highlights the fact that, while the way that schools are held accountable for educating students continues to evolve, the concept of school accountability appears to have become a mainstay feature of public-school education in the United States. Given this circumstance, there exists a need for schools to adopt a protocol that enables them to address, head on, the school accountability phenomenon. As was noted above, the response-to-intervention framework is an example of one such protocol.

Face Validity

Face validity refers to the extent that a procedure appears to make sense for its stated purpose. In the case of a RTI framework, it involves a subjective judgement as to whether the framework is considered to be a well-reasoned approach to address relevant matters such as more accurately identifying students with specific learning disabilities and ensuring that the most effective instruction possible is presented to each student in a school. The fact that 70 percent of school districts report that at least one of its schools have adopted a response-to-intervention framework can be cited as evidence of its face validity.

Yet, given that face validity is based upon a subjective judgement it is understandable that some will conclude that, in the absence of strong empirical evidence in support of the framework, it is no more than a theoretical exercise that, in practice, overtaxes a school's resources. The follow-up question that needs to be asked and answered is, "If not RTI, then what?"

RTI VERSUS SWPBIS VERSUS MTSS

As was noted above, the multi-component school reform effort that is the subject of this book has evolved over time. One aspect of this evolution is the use of different names for the same effort. By understanding this evolution, you will be prepared to assimilate information from related sources that you might consult about this topic as well as know why the use of the term "RTI framework" has been settled upon for this book.

Historically the terms RTI and *SWPBIS* have been used to describe frameworks that were associated with two somewhat different aspects of school programming: mastery of targeted academic content and displays of appropriate social behavior. RTI is the term that has referred to a multi-tier framework that addresses students' acquisition of academic content. In particular, initial response-to-intervention frameworks were associated with beginning reading instruction. SWPBIS has referred to multi-tier frameworks that focused on teaching students how to engage in appropriate social behaviors while at school.

As discussions about these frameworks progressed a number of authors noted the interrelationship that exists between students' displays of appropriate school social behaviors and their mastery of targeted academic skills.[21] A simple explanation of this relationship is that there exists a relatively low probability that students will master targeted academic content in chaotic instructional environments, meaning ones in which one or more students are engaging in inappropriate social behaviors that significantly disrupt the teacher's presentation of instruction and interfere with students' abilities to learn.[22]

In an attempt to address this inter-relatedness, some authors proposed the creation and use of what they called integrated multi-tier frameworks that consisted of protocols for simultaneously and efficiently addressing students' mastery of academic content and school social behavior. Still another term, Multi-Tier System of Support, has been coined to specify that some form of a multi-tier framework is being used but is not being identified as an RTI framework, SWPBIS framework, or some form of an integrated multi-tier framework.

In this book the term "RTI framework" is used to refer to the general concept of a multi-tier protocol that addresses students' mastery of academic skills or school social behavior, or both simultaneously, since this captures the essence of the premise of each framework. This premise is that school personnel need to proceed with educating students based on how they respond to the interventions provided. Furthermore, educating students encompasses the teaching of academic content as well as school social behavior since it is no longer a generally accepted maxim that students simply intuit how to engage in appropriate social behavior when they are at school.

Yet, in a limited number of instances the information that is presented about the framework does refer to the framework as it was originally conceived, meaning a multi-tier protocol for addressing students' mastery of academic content. In these instances, the text makes it clear that this is the case (e.g., where there are references to an academically-focused response-to-intervention framework).

A BOTTOM-UP EXPLANATION OF THE
RESPONSE-TO-INTERVENTION FRAMEWORK

Given a lack of evidence to the contrary, as well as what has been reported regarding teacher training as a part of previous school reform efforts, it is not unreasonable to surmise that one reason why implementations of the framework are not being executed properly and are being ineffective is because of insufficient teacher training. In turn, this circumstance may be attributable to what has been referred to as a routine top-down approach to school reform.

This means that a school reform protocol has been developed and explained in a way that is meaningful to school administrators (e.g., principals) and those agencies (e.g., school districts, state education agencies) that oversee and direct the work of schools, but not necessarily to teachers. The framework has been characterized as this type of approach to school reform.

However, a key component of this framework, or any school reform effort, is the personnel who provide direct services to students. These personnel include, but certainly are not limited to, general and special education teachers, teacher assistants, speech pathologists, occupational therapists, and school psychologists. Thus, while references to the teacher's role in the framework predominate throughout this book, this role is also fulfilled by one of the aforementioned instructors.

Hence, the purpose of this book is to present a bottom-up approach for explaining the framework. Specifically, the content is presented from an instructor's point of view, particularly an instructor who is new to the profession (i.e., preservice teachers, Teach for America candidates, those who have obtained alternate route status). The focus is on the essential elements of the RTI framework at the classroom—and individual-student level. The intent is to provide you with a fundamental understanding of the framework and how your use of sound, fundamental interventions can enable you to successfully fill your role in the framework.

The key role that instructors play in the success of any school reform effort probably will remain constant. This state of affairs is highlighted by remarks made by a senior military officer regarding the role of junior front-line officers in the implementation of a battle plan. The senior officer remarked that when he participated in the creation of a master battle plan, he constantly asked himself whether the front-line officers would be able to clearly understand their role because the success or failure of the plan rested on this understanding.

Teachers are the front-line officers with respect to any plan for school reform, such as the response-to-intervention framework. The success of this school reform depends on the work of teachers.

SCHOOL ADMINISTRATION HIERARCHICAL SUPPORTS

A teacher's success within a response-to-intervention framework will, however, depend to a large degree on the work of those who hold higher-level administrative positions. Hence, a key contributor to a teacher's perspective about a particular RTI framework will be the tasks that will be performed by school administrators and personnel in higher level parent organizations (e.g., a school district's central office or state education agencies).

While some of the framework's multi-tier components can be implemented in a classroom without there being a schoolwide multi-tier intervention framework in place, classroom- and individual-student level services and supports tend to be much more effective when schoolwide services are in place. Examples of these services are when school building administrators provide coaching, ongoing and expert professional development, classroom-level and individual-student supports, facilitation structures such as data interpretation and the scheduling of Tier 2 and Tier 3 services, and active and overt leadership (e.g., coordinating services, conducting fidelity checks, hiring qualified personnel.[23, 24]

A COMPREHENSIVE AND DETAILED
EXPLANATION THAT IS NOT OVERWHELMING

This book presents a comprehensive, detailed explanation of the response-to-intervention framework in a way that is intended to inform the reader without crossing the line at the point where the book becomes exhaustively detailed and confusing. At times the subject matter is intentionally oversimplified for the sake of clarity. These instances are clearly identified.

This approach allows the book to serve as a solid starting point, or foundation, for a more in-depth exploration of the topic from a wide variety of perspectives (e.g., instructor versus school administrator). Its content is appropriate for first-year teachers and experienced instructors—both those who are new to the framework or who have first-hand experience with it but want to learn about it from a different perspective (such as the perspective of a different author or a bottom-up, rather than a top-down, explanation of the framework).

Chapter 1

WHY SHOULD YOU KNOW
ABOUT RESPONSE-TO-INTERVENTION?

Below are some of the reasons why any teacher needs to know about this framework are listed and discussed. Additionally, this discussion addresses why you will benefit from reading the content in this book even if you do not work in a school that implements a response-to-intervention framework.

1. Since its inception, the framework has expanded from being used primarily to address the Individuals with Disabilities Education Act's (IDEA)[25] special education eligibility requirements for students with a specific learning disability to a systems-level protocol for monitoring the performance of every student.[26] According to some, RTI has become a general education, rather than a special education, scheme.[27]

2. A sizable amount of controlled research on RTI has shown that its use increases the likelihood of achieving improved outcomes for students with significant academic and social behavior needs.[28,29,30] However, recent findings from evaluations of RTI in practice have shown that the implementation of the framework in authentic school settings is being hindered by the fact that it is not being implemented as designed, which is a problem known as procedural fidelity.[31] This circumstance highlights the need to provide sufficient training about the framework to relevant stakeholders, such as teachers.

3. More than 70 percent of school districts across the country incorporate a RTI framework in at least some classrooms.[32] Furthermore, a review of relevant state policies revealed that nearly every state education agency recommends the use of a RTI framework in its schools and districts. Yet, this review indicated that fewer than 10 percent of the states provided guidelines for the implementation of RTI.[33,34,35]

4. The framework has been referred to as having the potential to be the basis for true school reform in the United States.[36] This assertion has been made despite the fact that, to date, no experimental or quasi-experimental studies of the efficacy of the framework as a comprehensive, integrated system have been conducted.[37] Teachers need to learn about the framework from their perspective so that, in the absence of clear and convincing evidence, they can conclude whether the alleged potential of the RTI framework is worth pursuing.

5. The more knowledgeable you are about the framework the better equipped you will be to evaluate relevant research as well as the fidelity of the implementation of the framework in a school. If you are considering working in a school that claims to use a RTI framework, be prepared to ask questions about how it is constructed, and implemented, and the expectations for your role in it should you be hired.

6. As was noted previously, RTI is addressed tangentially in the federal legislation (i.e., the Individuals with Disabilities Education Improvement Act of 2004 [IDEIA])[38] and accompanying regulations that dictate the provision of special education services to children with disabilities. This legislation refers to the use of response-to-intervention procedures when identifying students with specific learning disabilities.[39] In the United States, as a condition of their employment in a public school, teachers must be cognizant of, and comply with, the IDEIA and its accompanying regulations.

7. Should you work in a school that is implementing a RTI framework, its use will serve as the basis for the work that most direct service providers will perform. The framework that is being used will drive the administration of your school, meaning the administrative tasks you must complete, as well as how you are expected to teach—and how you will do so in conjunction with your peers.

8. You will benefit from learning about the high-quality, scientifically-based instruction that is the foundation of the intervention services component of the framework. Arguably, this kind of instruction should be presented in every general education classroom, irrespective of whether a school is using a RTI framework. While others who have written about the framework routinely reference this type of instruction, they usually have not explained it in much detail. Chapters 2 and 3 present information to address this void.

9. Similarly, you will benefit from learning about the nuances of intense, small group and 1:1 instruction that characterizes RTI services that are provided subsequent to high-quality instruction in a general education classroom. The way that a school implements its framework may result in a general education teacher having to provide these subsequent services.

10. As stated earlier, the framework has face validity. In the present era of school accountability, any valid approach that purportedly results in a comprehensive accounting of every student's attainment of expected learning outcomes needs to be considered by a school's staff so that they can determine "what works" for their school. Thus, the framework may, at the very least, serve as a starting point for the creation of a school's intervention efforts on behalf of low achieving and at-risk students.

CHAPTER 1 COMPREHENSION CHECK

Now that you have finished reading the chapter, you should be able to:

- Write a description of response-to-intervention (RTI).
- List and describe the two essential components of an RTI framework.
- Explain the rationale for the tier intervention services that comprise an RTI framework.
- Explain the underlying fundamental premise of Tier 1 services in an RTI framework.
- List an RTI framework's five principles and four features.
- Discuss the origin of the RTI framework.
- Explain what is meant by the term "school accountability" and how it can be addressed with an RTI framework.
- List the names of two other multi-tier frameworks that are similar to an RTI framework in design and focus.
- List three reasons why a prospective teacher needs to know about RTI frameworks.

NOTES

1. Douglas Fuchs and Lynn S. Fuchs, "Critique of the National Evaluation of Response-to-intervention: A Case for Simpler Frameworks," Exceptional Children 83, no. 3 (2017): 255–268.

2. Erin A. Chaparro, Kathleen Ryan Jackson, Scott K. Baker, and Keith Smolkowski, "Effective Behavioural and Instructional Support Systems: An Integrated Approach to Behaviour and Academic Support at the District Level," *Advances in School Mental Health Promotion* 5, no. 3 (2012): 161–176, doi: 10.1080/1754730X.2012.707424.

3. Sharon Vaughn, Sylvia Linan-Thompson, and Peggy Hickman, "Response to Instruction as a Means of Identifying Students with Reading/Learning Disabilities," *Exceptional Children* 69, no. 4 (2003): 391–409.

4. Aaron C. Barnes and Jason E. Harlacher, "Clearing the Confusion: Response-to-Intervention as a Set of Principles," *Education and Treatment of Children* 31, no. 3 (2008): 417–431.

5. Rachel M. Stewart, Gregory J. Benner, Ronald C. Martella, and Nancy E. Marchand-Martella, "Three-Tier Models of Reading and Behavior: A Research Review," *Journal of Positive Behavior Interventions* 9, no. 4 (2007): 239–253.

6. Aaron C. Barnes and Jason E. Harlacher, "Clearing the Confusion: Response-to-Intervention as a Set of Principles," *Education and Treatment of Children* 31, no. 3 (2008): 417–431.

7. Individuals with Disabilities Education Improvement Act of 2004, 20 U. S. C. § 1400 et seq. (2004).

8. Jack M. Fletcher, Sally E. Shaywitz, Donald P. Shankweiler, Leonard Katz, Isabelle Y. Liberman, Karla K. Stuebing, David J. Francis, Anne E. Fowler, and Bennett A. Shaywitz, "Cognitive Profiles of Reading Disability: Comparisons of Discrepancy and Low Achievement Definitions," *Journal of Educational Psychology* 86, no. 1 (1994): 6.

9. B. R. Foorman, D. J. Francis, and J. M. Fletcher, "Growth of Phonological Processing Skills in Beginning Reading: The Lag versus Deficit Model Revisited," *Society for Research on Child Development*, (Indianapolis, IN, 1995).

10. Keith E. Stanovich and Linda S. Siegel, "Phenotypic Performance Profile of Children with Reading Disabilities: A Regression-Based Test of the Phonological-Core Variable-Difference Model," *Journal of Educational Psychology* 86, no. 1 (1994): 24.

11. Jack M. Fletcher, D. J. Francis, B. A. Shaywitz, B. R. Foorman, and S. E. Shaywitz, "Diagnostic Utility of Intelligence Testing and the Discrepancy Model for Children with Learn-

ing Disabilities: Historical Perspectives and Current Research," *Workshop on IQ Testing and Educational Decision Making*, National Research Council, Washington, DC, 1995.

12. Robin D. Morris, Karla K. Stuebing, Jack M. Fletcher, Sally E. Shaywitz, G. Reid Lyon, Donald P. Shankweiler, Leonard Katz, David J. Francis, and Bennett A. Shaywitz, "Subtypes of Reading Disability: Variability Around a Phonological Core," *Journal of Educational Psychology* 90, no. 3 (1998): 347.

13. Keith E. Stanovich, "The Sociopsychometrics of Learning Disabilities," *Journal of Learning Disabilities* 32, no. 4 (1999): 350–361.

14. Joseph K. Torgesen, S. Morgan, and C. Davis, "The Effects of Two Types of Phonological Awareness Training on Word Learning in Kindergarten Children," *Journal of Educational Psychology* 84, (1992): 364–370.

15. Frank R. Vellutino, Donna M. Scanlon, Edward R. Sipay, Sheila G. Small, Alice Pratt, RuSan Chen, and Martha B. Denckla, "Cognitive Profiles of Difficult-to-Remediate and Readily Remediated Poor Readers: Early Intervention as a Vehicle for Distinguishing Between Cognitive and Experiential Deficits as Basic Causes of Specific Reading Disability," *Journal of Educational Psychology* 88, no. 4 (1996): 601.

16. Douglas Fuchs and Lynn S. Fuchs, "Introduction to Response-to-intervention: What, Why, and How Valid is It?" *Reading Research Quarterly* 41, no. 1 (2006): 93–99.

17. Ibid.

18. Individuals with Disabilities Education Act of 1975, 20 U. S. C. § 1400 et seq. (1975).

19. No Child Left Behind Act of 2001, PL 107–110, 115 Stat. 1425, 20 U.S.C. § 6301 et seq.

20. Every Student Succeeds Act, Pub L. No. 114–95, § 1, 129 Stat. 1802. (2015).

21. Jack M. Fletcher, Sally E. Shaywitz, Donald P. Shankweiler, Leonard Katz, Isabelle Y. Liberman, Karla K. Stuebing, David J. Francis, Anne E. Fowler, and Bennett A. Shaywitz, "Cognitive Profiles of Reading Disability: Comparisons of Discrepancy and Low Achievement Definitions," *Journal of Educational Psychology* 86, no. 1 (1994): 6.

22. Kathleen Lynne Lane, Erik W. Carter, Abbie Jenkins, Lauren Dwiggins, and Kathryn Germer, "Supporting Comprehensive, Integrated, Three-Tiered Models of Prevention in Schools: Administrators' Perspectives," *Journal of Positive Behavior Interventions* 17, no. 4 (2015): 209–222.

23. George Sugai and Robert R. Horner, "A Promising Approach for Expanding and Sustaining School-Wide Positive Behavior Support," *School Psychology Review* 35, no. 2 (2006): 245.

24. Brandi Simonsen, Sarah Fairbanks, Amy Briesch, Diane Myers, and George Sugai, "Evidence-Based Practices in Classroom Management: Considerations for Research to Practice," *Education and Treatment of Children* (2008): 351–380.

25. Individuals with Disabilities Education Act of 1975, 20 U. S. C. § 1400 et seq. (1975).

26. Mitchell L. Yell, *The Law and Special Education*, third edition, ed. Jeffrey Johnston, (New Jersey: Pearson Education, Inc. 2012).

27. Sarah D. Sparks, "Study: RTI Practice Falls Short of Promise," *Education Week* 35, no. 12 (2015): 1. Available at http://www.edweek.org/ew/articles/2015/11/11/study-rti-practice-falls-short-of-promise.html.

28. Douglas Fuchs, Lynn S. Fuchs, and Donald L. Compton, "Smart RTI: A Next-Generation Approach to Multilevel Prevention," *Exceptional Children* 78, no. 3 (2012): 263–279.

29. Edward S. Shapiro, "Tiered Instruction and Intervention in a Response-to-Intervention Model," *RTI Action Network* 381 (2014). Available at http://www.rtinetwork.org/essential/tieredinstruction/tiered-instruction-and-intervention-rti-model.

30. Sharon Vaughn and Elizabeth A. Swanson, "Special Education Research Advances Knowledge in Education," *Exceptional Children* 82, no. 1 (2015): 11–24.

31. Douglas Fuchs and Lynn S. Fuchs, "Introduction to Response-to-intervention: What, Why, and How Valid is It?" *Reading Research Quarterly* 41, no. 1 (2006): 93–99.

32. Sarah D. Sparks, "Study: RTI Practice Falls Short of Promise," *Education Week* 35, no. 12 (2015): 1. Available at http://www.edweek.org/ew/articles/2015/11/11/study-rti-practice-falls-short-of-promise.html.

33. Sarah V. Arden, Allison Gruner Gandhi, Rebecca Zumeta Edmonds, and Louis Daniel-son, "Toward More Effective Tiered Systems: Lessons from National Implementation Efforts," *Exceptional Children* 83, no. 3 (2017): 269–280.

34. Laura Boynton Hauerwas, Rachel Brown, and Amy N. Scott, "Specific Learning Dis-ability and Response-to-intervention: State-Level Guidance," *Exceptional Children* 80, no. 1 (2013): 101–120.

35. Tina M. Hudson and Robert G. McKenzie, "Evaluating the Use of RTI to Identify SLD: A Survey of State Policy, Procedures, Data Collection, and Administrator Perceptions," *Con-temporary School Psychology* 20, no. 1 (2016): 31–45.

36. R. H. Horner, G. Sugai, A. W. Todd, T. Lewis-Palmer, L. Bambara, and L. Kern, *Individualized Supports for Students with Problem Behaviors: Designing Positive Behavior Plans*, (2005).

37. Lynn S. Fuchs, Douglas Fuchs, Allison Gandhi, and Rebecca Zumeta Edmonds, RTI Hits Adolescence—Will It Make It to Adulthood? A Case for Cautious Optimism, Center on Response-to-intervention, American Institutes for Research, 2016. Available at https://rti4success.org/sites/default/files/RTIAdolescence.pdf.

38. Individuals with Disabilities Education Improvement Act of 2004, 20 U. S. C. § 1400 et seq. (2004).

39. Mitchell L. Yell, *The Law and Special Education*, third edition, ed. Jeffrey Johnston (New Jersey: Pearson Education, Inc., 2012).

Chapter Two

Tier 1 Services

Essential Elements of High-Quality Instruction in the General Education Classroom

OVERVIEW

In this chapter you will learn about the high-quality, scientifically-based instruction that is to be provided in Tier 1 of a RTI framework. Key points from the chapter include the following:

In any RTI framework, Tier 1 serves as the foundation of the tiered intervention services component and consists of the presentation of high-quality, scientifically-based instruction in general education classrooms.

High-quality instruction can be defined in a number of ways. In this chapter it is operationally defined so that school personnel can readily make changes to aspects of Tier 1 services when they determine that effective instruction has not been presented and that, because of this circumstance, one or more features of high-quality instruction needs to be addressed.

High-quality instruction is a multi-dimensional construct that involves the appropriate design and operation of a classroom, successful time management, a focus on core curriculum content, the presentation of effective instructional strategies, and the use of valid and reliable assessments.

A school's curriculum is a comprehensive listing of the knowledge and skills that students are expected to learn via the instruction they are presented at school.

Broadly speaking, a school's curriculum addresses academic and social behaviors.

A curriculum's academic content refers to the knowledge and skills that pertain to traditional disciplines (i.e., math, science, English/language arts,

social studies) and the curriculum's content that concerns school social behaviors refers to how students act so as to share space appropriately with
others across all school-related environments.

Effective instruction is defined as instruction that results in a student
demonstrating mastery of targeted learning objectives.

OVERVIEW OF HIGH-QUALITY, SCIENTIFICALLY-BASED
INSTRUCTION IN THE GENERAL EDUCATION CLASSROOM

The content presented in chapter 1 explained the general parameters, or
features, of any RTI framework. The features include:

1. The use of screening and progress monitoring assessments as a means
   of obtaining data that will be evaluated to decide the intervention tier
   in which a student will be placed
2. The use of multiple tiers of intervention, with the exact number of
   tiers varying across RTI frameworks
3. The first tier of every RTI framework consisting of the presentation of
   high-quality, scientifically-based instruction in the general education
   classroom. Subsequent tiers involve changes to the intensity and nature of the instruction that is presented. One of these tiers will account
   for the provision of special education services.

Tier 1 services are the focus of the content that is presented in this chapter
and chapter 3. Tier 1 of every RTI framework consists of the presentation of
high-quality, scientifically-based instruction in the general education classroom. One caveat to this statement is that the teaching of appropriate school
social behavior will occur in the general education classroom as well as
across a school's campus and other locations that are determined to be a part
of a school's jurisdiction, such as a school bus. However, for the sake of
clarity, in this book the discussion of Tier 1 services will focus on the instruction that is presented in a general education classroom.

This instruction is initially presented to every student and is expected to
result in 75–80 percent of them attaining expected learning outcomes. Regardless the total number of tiers in any particular response-to-intervention
framework, the general features of Tier 1 services are the same: high-quality,
scientifically-based instruction that is presented to every student in the general education classroom.

This chapter addresses the concept of high-quality instruction in two
ways. First, an operational definition for the term is put forth. Second, an
explanation is offered regarding why Tier 1 RTI instruction must simultaneously address academic skills and school social behaviors in order for high-

quality instruction to be presented. This explanation supports the reasoning that was offered previously regarding why the term RTI framework is used in this book. Afterwards, chapter 3 explains what is meant by scientifically-based instruction and addresses relevant issues about this instruction in Tier 1 of the framework.

TIER 1 AS THE FOUNDATION OF ANY RTI FRAMEWORK

While the number of tiers in a response-to-intervention framework can vary, the foundation of the first tier in any framework is the presentation of what is referred to as high quality, scientifically-based instruction in the general education classroom. Thus, this instruction functions as the reference point for the subsequent intervention services that are provided in the other tiers. Consequently, it is imperative that the terms "high-quality instruction" and "scientifically-based instruction" are operationally defined so that one can determine if, in fact, this type of instruction has been provided in a general education classroom or, if not, what can be done so that this instruction is presented.

An *operational definition* is one that defines a concept in observable, measurable terms such that two or more individuals can agree upon its existence when they see it. You need to know how your school operationally defines high-quality instruction so that you will know what you need to do to demonstrate that you are presenting it.

Remember from the explanation in chapter 1 of the tiered intervention component of a response-to-intervention framework, that it must be demonstrated that a student was provided high-quality instruction prior to concluding that a student's lack of expected, or hoped for, progress in the general education classroom needs to be addressed in another tier. Conversely, if it is determined that high-quality instruction had not been presented, then instead of moving a student to Tier 2 other efforts would be made to enhance the instruction that is being presented in the general education classroom. For instance, professional development would be provided to the general education teacher with the intent of improving upon the work that she is performing in the classroom such that it can be considered to be high-quality instruction.

The various observable, measurable elements that combine to result in the provision of high-quality instruction are subject to debate. In fact, some who have provided guidance, for either the presentation of effective instruction or the implementation of an RTI framework, have referenced the need to provide high quality instruction but did not even attempt to explicitly define it. [1]

Yet, it is questionable how a school can use a response-to-intervention framework effectively if its personnel cannot readily agree as to whether students have been presented this instruction since it serves as the basis for all other tiered intervention services. Altogether the information that is presented in this chapter and chapter 3 is offered as one operational definition for high-quality instruction.

OPERATIONALLY DEFINING HIGH-QUALITY
INSTRUCTION: GENERAL CONSIDERATIONS

A Continuum of Quality Instruction and Its Subjective Interpretation

Perhaps the main challenge to operationally defining high-quality instruction is that the term implies that it exists relative to a baseline standard. If the term quality instruction is simply defined as effective instruction, meaning instruction that results in students attaining expected learning outcomes, it is reasonable to conclude that this instruction can be described in terms of a continuum on which effective instruction refers to the percentage of students who attained the expected learning outcomes.

For instance, this continuum would include basic, or relatively low-quality, effective instruction that results in the majority of students (i.e., at least 51 percent, and up to 64 percent) attaining expected learning outcomes. Medium quality instruction could then be defined in terms of a higher percentage (65–74 percent) of students attaining these outcomes. High-quality instruction might then be defined in terms of an even higher percentage (75 percent or more) of students not only attaining these outcomes but perhaps also doing so in less time than the students who had received low or medium quality instruction.

Below the guidance that an elementary school principal gave to his first-year teachers is offered as an example of how quality instruction can be viewed as existing along a continuum, especially when it is not operationally defined and is permitted to be left to each individual's subjective interpretation.

The principal told his first-year teachers—who were assigned to teach reading, math, science, and social studies in their classrooms—to present effective instruction in each academic discipline but to choose one of these disciplines and spend several years designing teaching techniques so that, at the end of that time, the teacher would have developed what she believed to be a first-class instructional program. At this point in time the teacher would maintain this program and then move on to developing another first-class instructional program in one of the three other academic disciplines. She would then continue this process until she had developed first-class instructional programs in each of the four academic disciplines.

The upside of this principal's perspective regarding the type of instruction that is presented in a classroom is that it can be made to be more effective. One way of explaining this perspective is that the principal believed that a teacher could present good instruction that could be improved upon so that it became very good instruction and, ultimately, great instruction. This perspective is explained in the next section with respect to high-quality instruction.

Objectively Defining High-Quality Instruction Only in Terms of Student Outcomes

Considering how the response-to-intervention framework has been described in terms of the percentage of students who will attain expected learning outcomes in each of the intervention tiers, one might be tempted to define high-quality instruction accordingly. This approach would define *high-quality instruction* as instruction presented in the general education classroom that results in 75–80 percent of the students attaining expected learning outcomes.

One problem with this definition is that it is not an operational definition. Two individuals could not observe the instruction and agree that it consisted of observable, measurable components that had been identified as part of the concept. Rather, the student outcome data would allow for a retrospective conclusion that high-quality instruction had been presented. However, the outcome data may be more the result of the students having above average innate abilities that enabled them to attain the expected outcomes despite the fact that high-quality instruction had not been presented.

This problem with defining high-quality instruction as such readily leads to the identification of a second problem with defining high-quality instruction in this manner. That is, doing so does not allow for one to critically examine how the instruction that is being presented in a classroom could be systematically changed when fewer than 75–80 percent of the students did not attain expected learning outcomes.

Furthermore, even when this percentage of students did attain these outcomes, a similar examination of the instruction could not be conducted so that the instruction could be improved upon in a way that enabled an even greater percentage of students to attain the outcomes. Going back to the previous discussion about a continuum of quality instruction, this latter type of instruction might be referred to using the term "exceptionally high-quality instruction."

Implying That Scientific-Based Instruction is Always High-Quality Instruction; Causal Relationship Between High-Quality and Evidence-Based Instruction

Discussions about high-quality instruction in a response-to-intervention framework have been closely linked to what has been referred to as scientifically-based instruction. This linkage—which results from references to Tier 1 services as being comprised of high-quality, scientifically-based instruction—may lead one to conclude that the use of scientifically-based instruction, in and of itself, is high-quality instruction.

Scientifically-based instruction refers to the use of research to validate effective interventions. Constant time delay is an example of a scientifically-based instructional strategy for teaching students with disabilities to read high frequency words. However, its use in a chaotic classroom may not prove to be effective, which means that just referencing the use of scientifically-based instruction does not mean that high-quality instruction has been presented. Perhaps what can be said is that the use of scientifically-based instruction increases the probability that high-quality instruction will be presented. As is the case regarding high-quality instruction, scientifically-based instruction must be operationally defined.

Chapter 3 explains the meaning of scientifically-based instruction and a synonymous term that is used more often: evidence-based practice. The relevance of both terms to a response-to-intervention framework is explained as well.

The discussion presented next is offered as one way to define the features that would characterize a general education classroom in which high-quality instruction is presented. Importantly, the way these features are defined readily allows for the general education classroom to be reconfigured should a student who is in it not demonstrate mastery of the general education curriculum (e.g., distractions could be eliminated, the amount of active student responding could be increased, etc.). Moreover, it establishes a reference point for determining how the services that are provided in Tier 2 and Tier 3 are markedly different from, yet directly related to, the services that are provided in the general education classroom.

HIGH-QUALITY INSTRUCTION: EFFECTIVE AND MULTI-DIMENSIONAL

High-Quality Instruction is Effective Instruction

While high-quality instruction cannot be defined solely in terms of students' attainment of expected learning outcomes, its definition must account, in part, for its relationship to these outcomes. Doing so is consistent with other authors' explanations of how the basis for the RTI framework's tiered intervention services is the presentation of high-quality instruction in the general education classroom such that 75–80 percent of the students attain expected outcomes.

When this occurs, this instruction can also be characterized as effective instruction. Effective instruction is defined as instruction that results in a student demonstrating mastery of the targeted learning objective. Learning objectives are statements that describe either the academic or school social behaviors students are to be able to perform after receiving effective instruction.

Since the framework can be used to address both academic and non-academic skills, references to students' "attainment of expected outcomes" is often used since it encompasses both academic and school social behaviors. Consequently, throughout this book the term effective instruction is used interchangeably with high-quality instruction, particularly when doing so allows for a clearer presentation of the content.

High-Quality Instruction is Multi-Dimensional

As was noted during the previous discussion regarding the presumed relationship between high-quality and scientifically-based instruction, high-quality instruction involves more than just the instructional strategy a teacher uses at the point in time when she conducts a lesson. This instruction results from additional components that include work a teacher performs before and after presenting a lesson. Thus, high-quality instruction is a multidimensional construct. The various dimensions of instruction that intertwine to result in high-quality instruction include the following:

1. A safe, orderly classroom that is conducive to the presentation of effective instruction
2. Successful time management
3. Presentation of effective instructional strategies, which include both what are referred to as fundamental universal principles of effective teaching and strategies that are specific to an academic discipline, such as the teaching of reading or math. In both cases the strategies are evidence-based practices.
4. A focus on core curriculum content plus an appropriate pacing guide (i.e., a relevant scope and sequence)
5. The use of valid, reliable assessments to measure students' mastery of the grade-level standards in the core curriculum and students' demonstration of appropriate school social behaviors

Before discussing each of these components in detail, definitions for key terms that are used in this discussion and throughout chapters 3–5 are presented. Knowing the meanings of these key terms will enhance your understanding of the discussions.

KEY TERMS DEFINED

Sometimes in the field of education multiple definitions are offered for a single term or phrase. One example of this phenomenon is the multiple definitions that have been offered for the term curriculum. Furthermore, different terms can, in some people's minds, refer to the same concept. For instance, some educators think the terms explicit instruction, systematic instruction, and direct instruction are synonymous. Altogether these circumstances can lead to confusion.

While this book's glossary provides definitions for a wide variety of noteworthy terms and phrases that are used in this book, below some key terms and concepts are listed and defined. As you read the content below remain mindful of the fact that the purpose of this section is not to get you to agree with how the key vocabulary in this book have been defined. Rather, the purpose is to make transparent to you the meanings of these key vocabulary. To be able to comprehend the overall meaning of the connected text you must first understand the meanings of individual words.

Effective instruction. Instruction that results in a student demonstrating mastery of the targeted learning objective. Throughout this book references to effective instruction are made more often than references to high quality instruction since (a) effective instruction results from high quality instruction and (b) effective instruction is the goal of the intervention services that are provided at each tier of the framework.

Learning objective. A statement which describes the knowledge or skill from the curriculum that the student will acquire after being presented effective instruction. This statement includes (a) the student's name; (b) an observable, measurable explanation of the knowledge or skill he will acquire; (c) the conditions under which the student will acquire the knowledge or skill; and, (d) the criteria for mastery. For example, when presented with ten index cards on which are written high frequency words, Jakarei will read each word correctly within two seconds across three consecutive daily probes.

Curriculum. A comprehensive listing of the knowledge and skills that students are expected to learn via the instruction they are presented at school.

Learning. A relatively permanent change in behavior resulting from experience (i.e., a change in behavior that results from receiving instruction). This definition differentiates learning from other changes in behavior that are the result of some factor other than teaching. An example is physical maturation. Whereas a student can be taught how to add two single-digit numbers, after learning how to pick up a bag of sand he cannot be taught how to pick up a ten-pound bag instead of a five-pound bag if he has not physically matured to the point of being able to do so.

Mastery. A student is said to have demonstrated mastery when she has acquired the knowledge or skill that is defined in a learning objective in accordance with the established criterion for correct responding (e.g., reading ten high frequency words within thirty seconds across three consecutive assessment sessions or complying with all of the rules for appropriate behavior while eating lunch in the cafeteria on 95 percent of the days during a nine-week grading period).

Instructional strategy. The planned actions a teacher executes when she presents a lesson. Synonymous terms include teaching procedure, teaching strategy, and teaching method.

Teaching. The actions, or behaviors, a teacher exhibits to enable her students to master their learning objectives and, hence, their curriculum. Teaching involves imparting knowledge and skills to others.

It is important to note how teaching differs from providing students with accommodations or modifications since a response-to-intervention framework focuses much more so on the use of the former. Accommodations are changes to the conditions under which a student is expected to acquire knowledge or perform an academic skill, rather than an alteration of the standard that has been set for performance—which is a modification.

Accommodations may include, but are not necessarily limited to, the time that a student is given to complete a task, the manner in which the task is presented to the student (e.g., in writing rather than an oral presentation), the mode of responding that is required from the student (e.g., typewritten rather than handwritten answers), and the arrangement of the setting in which the task is to be performed (e.g., in a small rather than large group).

The purpose for providing an accommodation is to ensure that a student's performance is a valid reflection of his ability to perform a targeted skill. Accommodations are provided to allow for an equitable, as opposed to advantageous, situation for a student.

Efficient instruction. Efficient instruction is effective instruction that, relative to one or more other means of presenting effective instruction, requires less time, teacher effort, or financial or tangible resources. This concept is relevant to Tier 2 services and the use of a standard treatment program versus a problem-solving protocol. These topics are discussed in chapter 4.

DIMENSIONS OF HIGH-QUALITY INSTRUCTION

Each of the dimensions of high-quality instruction that were identified above are explained in detail below. As you read each explanation think about how the dimension is defined in observable, measurable terms such that the dimension could be reconfigured in a way that could be measured in terms of effective instruction.

High-Quality Instruction: Environmental Arrangement and Management

The classrooms within a school are the locations where teachers and students spend the most time interacting. It stands to reason, therefore, that one component of high-quality instruction is the creation of a safe, orderly general education classroom that facilitates teaching and learning.

The term *environmental arrangement* is used to refer to the appropriate arrangement of this and any other location where a response-to-intervention framework's tiered intervention services are provided. Since the focus of Tier 1 intervention services is high-quality instruction in a general education classroom, the information that is presented below pertains to this location. For the sake of clarity, think about a typical, traditional general education classroom in which twenty to thirty or more students receive instruction from one teacher. This is called a large group arrangement and is the focus of the information that is presented in this section.

The importance of creating safe, orderly classrooms has been highlighted by research that has established a positive correlation between students' engagement in appropriate school social behaviors and their attainment of expected academic outcomes.[2,3] Furthermore, research has documented that, in many instances, the same types of instructional strategies can be used to teach both.[4]

Anecdotally, others[5] highlighted how students' displays of appropriate school social behavior is related to the provision of effective instruction by discussing the implications of a relationship that might exist between the incarceration rates of youth who also are not proficient readers. These authors made the point that teaching students to be successful readers may or may not ultimately impact their incarceration rates. Yet, it was reasonable to conclude that if these students engaged in inappropriate, disruptive behaviors while someone was attempting to teach them how to read, this circumstance certainly would decrease the probability that they, as well as their classmates, would learn how to do so.

Below, some of the issues you will need to address to be able to create and operate an environment that supports the presentation of effective instruction, are listed and discussed. The issues are discussed in sufficient detail to enable you to develop an understanding of their importance as well acquire some knowledge about how to address them. These issues highlight the fact that universal effective teaching practices include both interventions that are defined as changes to the environment that set the occasion for the presentation of effective instruction as well as instructional strategies that primarily involve the demonstration of behaviors by the teacher that have been shown to result in students' attainment of targeted learning outcomes.

As you consider each issue, be mindful of the fact that establishing an appropriate environmental arrangement is a dynamic, as opposed to static, undertaking. Factors such as (a) a change in the class roster or (b) your incorporation of new instructional strategies (e.g., cooperative learning groups) may result in you having to change the way you have arranged the environment. While you do not want to waste time addressing this topic, you do need to recognize that it may present a reoccurring demand on your time that you must address to be able to present high quality instruction.

1. Establish clear lines of sight for both the teacher and the students. Clear lines of sight enable teachers to manage students' displays of appropriate school social behaviors and assess their understanding of a lesson. Research has shown that teachers who conduct a visual scan of the entire classroom every one to two minutes have students who engage in appropriate school social behaviors more often.[6] When scanning the classroom, the teacher can provide either the entire class or individual students with behavior-specific praise, thereby reinforcing them for displays of these behaviors.

    a. Providing students with clear lines of sight allows them to both see any person or item that is central to the presentation of instruction and attend in a way that does not disrupt the lesson. A disruption refers to any event that draws attention to itself and impedes the ongoing flow of activities in a classroom. Thus, if a student gets out of his seat and moves about the room to improve his line of sight or leans to one side of his desk to do so, but also inadvertently bumps into another student, these actions may function as disruptions.

    b. Numerous techniques can be used to check for student's understanding of the lesson. A very simple one is interpreting students' facial expressions. The display of a grimace or frown may indicate that a student does not understand the targeted learning outcome. A more objective approach to assessing students' understanding is for the teacher to periodically pose comprehension questions and have students respond simultaneously but by way of a response mode that can be interpreted individually (e.g., in response to a true or false question each student either shows a thumbs up to indicate their answer is true or a thumbs down to indicate their answer is false).

2. Take necessary steps to ensure that the climate is conducive to effective instruction. A student may not be able to focus on the teacher's instruction when he is uncomfortable because of some feature of the classroom's climate. These features may include inadequate lighting (too much light or darkness), an uncomfortable temperature setting (too hot or cold), or a structural defect (e.g., water dripping from the ceiling or snow or rain being blown through a window's seal).

   While a teacher may not be able to control these features, she needs to be mindful of their potential impact on instruction as well as how she might be able to intervene to mitigate them (e.g., permit students who say it is too bright to wear a baseball cap or students who say they are cold to wear a sweater).

3. Create protocols for managing high traffic areas. Students frequent some areas of a classroom more than others, such as the pencil sharpener, trash can, the hanging drape with pockets where calculators are stored, and the tray where they are to turn in their homework and the assignments they complete while in class. A teacher must strategically locate these areas such that they are both out of students' direct lines of sight and easily accessible. These arrangements will serve as antecedent-based interventions that increase the probability that a student will not disrupt a lesson when accessing a high traffic area.

   To assist in the management of these areas, the teacher should establish routines and set rules for accessing them. A routine for entering an Algebra 1 class may be for students to first get a calculator from the storage bin, sit in their assigned seats and then begin working on a test prep question that is written on the classroom's whiteboard. An example of a rule for accessing a high traffic area would be that only one person at a time can be out of their seat to use the pencil sharpener.

4. Limit potential distractions. A teacher wants students to attend to the aspects of a lesson that she deems to be most important, such as her modeling how to solve a long division problem or how to identify key locations on a map during a geography lesson. When a student is distracted this means he is attending to some other aspect of the environment. If the teacher then has to redirect the student's attention, the distraction would serve as a disruption. Teachers can take a number of actions to limit distractions, such as (a) positioning portable dividers in locations that eliminate visual distractions and (b) controlling for

auditory distractions by only permitting students to use a printer when doing so would not serve as a potential auditory distraction.

5. Plan for both the use of floor and wall space. Teachers need to address different issues that are specific to both the use of floor space and wall space which, for the purpose of this discussion, includes a classroom's ceiling space. Yet, they need to coordinate their design of floor and wall space in order to create an organized classroom.

   a. Regarding floor space, teachers need to consider the amount that is available and its configuration when planning their students' seating arrangement and the placement of classroom furniture, such as bookshelves. Two primary considerations that were addressed above will be ensuring clear lines of sight and an efficient traffic flow.

   b. Teachers will need to contemplate several issues when planning for the use of wall space. First, they need to decide whether this space will be used to present instruction, enhance the classroom's organization, display decorations, or reinforce students via displays of their work or performance data. Examples of how a teacher can use wall space to present instruction include creating a word wall comprised of key vocabulary from a novel the students are reading or the order of operations that need to be followed to solve an algebra problem. To enhance the classroom's organization the teacher may post a weekly and daily schedule as well as a list of the activities that will take place in a lesson.

   c. Decorations could consist of students' artwork or seasonal exhibitions that pertain to upcoming holidays. Displays of students' work and performance data could include an exemplary essay and a line graph that depicts the number of sight words a student has mastered during the current grading period.

   d. Second, if portable floor dividers are placed throughout the classroom, the teacher will have to decide if they will be used like fixed wall space. Third, the teacher will have to decide whether she will allow mobiles to hang from the ceiling. Just like other fixtures that are placed on walls, these mobiles could be informative, decorative, or reinforcing. However, care must be taken to prevent them from serving as a distraction.

   e. The overarching consideration when deciding how to design wall space is to ensure that its design contributes to, rather than detracts from, the presentation of high-quality instruction. The space that is available on the walls that surround a classroom will exceed the room's floor space. Hence, its use warrants considerable attention.

6. Ensure that instructional materials are nearby and ready for use. Teachers need to position instructional materials so that they are readily accessible and usable. Doing so allows for effective behavior management and the efficient use of allocated time.

   a. When instructional materials are very close by the location where the teacher will present the instruction, she can continue to monitor students' behavior while she seamlessly accesses needed materials. Additionally, the teacher will not waste instructional time as might be the case when she has to walk to another place in the room to get needed materials.
   b. Likewise, instructional time will be lost if a teacher has to prepare materials that were not made ready in advance of a lesson. This would occur when a teacher has to take time away from a lesson to make copies of a handout that pertains to a lecture or worksheets students will be required to complete.

7. Consider how you will incorporate existing fixtures. Teachers either will not be permitted to move some fixtures in the environment or cannot move them given the school's design. Examples might include storage cabinets, electrical outlets, ports for connecting computers to the internet, chalkboards, countertops, and sinks. Teachers will have to plan for these fixtures "as is" in conjunction with all of the other considerations mentioned here.

8. Recognize the potential influence of a classroom's aesthetics on students' behavior. This aspect of an environmental arrangement refers to its overall look and feel. Simply stated, an appropriately lit, colorful, well-organized, climate-controlled room that exudes a sense of calm can set the occasion for displays of appropriate student behavior since students will be more likely to want to come to the room to work. Conversely, a poorly lit, uncomfortable, disorganized room could result in students neither wanting to enter or remain in it irrespective of the fact that they otherwise enjoy engaging in the instruction that is presented.

9. Development and use of routines that support instruction. Classroom routines are repeated sequences of actions. Routines make efficient use of allocated time and establish behavioral momentum.

a. An example of a routine that makes use of allocated time and, therefore, supports the instruction that is presented in a math class is as follows: upon entering the classroom a student obtains a practice test question from the teacher, who is standing at the doorway; the student then gets her calculator from its storage pocket that is on a curtain that is hanging on a wall in the rear of the classroom; next the student goes to her assigned seat and situates her belongings; afterward she places her homework in the "Finished Tasks" box that is located on the teacher's desk; finally, the student returns to her seat and answers the practice test question.

b. Behavioral momentum refers to the fact that students are more likely to continue to engage in appropriate behaviors after already exhibiting several or more appropriate behaviors in a row.

High-Quality Instruction: Successful Time Management

Arguably one of a teacher's most valuable resources is the time she has been allocated to teach. The presentation of high-quality instruction depends, in part, on a teacher being cognizant of this time and properly managing it.

The breadth, or scope, of the curriculum that must be taught highlights the importance of proper time management. Those involved in curriculum design know that a noteworthy challenge is settling upon a curriculum's content. One reason for this circumstance is one can readily identify more knowledge and skills that students probably should be taught than there is time available to teach them. Ultimately factors including available funding, the length of the school year, and the length of each school day set an upper limit with respect to how much content can be taught. Thus, teachers need to properly manage their allocated time to achieve this upper limit.

Mindful of this fact, a teacher does not want to lower this limit by improperly managing her allocated time. Likewise, students must have the same commitment. A teacher can take steps to properly manage her allocated time in a way that is designed to meet each student's needs, but each student also has the responsibility to take full advantage of the teacher's efforts by remaining appropriately engaged during a lesson.

Furthermore, one distinction between the tiers of intervention services in an RTI framework is the amount of time a student receives instruction. One way the concept of increased intensity of instruction is defined in the framework is allocating more time to the presentation of instruction that pertains to learning outcomes students have not attained after receiving only Tier 1 services.

Others[7] devised a way to conceptualize the time that is available for instruction each school day. Their model serves as the basis for the discussion presented below.

The term allotted time refers to the total amount of time in one school day that is available for teaching. If a school day begins at 8 a.m. and ends at 3:30 p.m., and the students are permitted thirty minutes to eat lunch and a total of thirty minutes to change classes during the day, then the allotted time would be six hours and thirty minutes.

Allocated time is the amount of time that has been designated to teach subject matter content, such as English/language arts, math, science, and social studies. Within the amount of allotted time previously identified, in an elementary school ninety minutes may be allocated for English/language arts instruction and seventy-five minutes for mathematics instruction. In a high school that uses what is referred to as a block schedule, ninety-four minutes may be allocated for each class period. This means each subject area teacher would be allocated ninety-four minutes for each period during which she taught her subject, such as world history.

In many instances, state departments of education establish the minimum amount of time that must be allocated each day for certain subject area instruction. Some schools then further dictate to teachers the curriculum content they are to teach on a designated day as well as the amount of time they are to spend teaching each subtopic. In these instances, teachers have been presented what is referred to as a pacing guide.

Engaged time is defined as the amount of time during the allocated time when instruction is being presented that a student attends to the instruction. In turn, the term academic learning time refers to the amount of time that a student is taught relevant content that is at his instructional level.

In Tier 1 students receive content area instruction during allocated time every day school is in session, which typically is five days per week during the months that comprise the school year. The general education teacher manages allocated time in accordance with the subject matter area curriculum's scope and sequence that she must follow within a subject matter area. As was noted above, some schools strictly manage this task via a pacing guide.

Within this allocated time, when she is presenting whole class instruction, she may use various strategies to maximize students' engaged time, such as (a) presenting an attention directive, which might consist of a statement—such as "Eyes up"—that directs the students to attend to the teacher; (b) having students use response cards, which are small cards on which an answer is displayed and which a student holds up to indicate his response to a teacher's comprehension check question; and, (c) using a model-lead-test routine that involves having all students respond at the same time when the teacher presents the lead, or what is also called the guided practice, portion of the lesson. Having all students respond at the same time is known as choral responding.

Also, she may present some amount of differentiated instruction within a large group lesson to maximize students' academic learning time. These strategies might be supplemented with others, such as learning centers, cooperative peer groups, and teacher-led small group instruction with the intent of increasing either the students' engaged or academic learning time, or both.

Tier 2 and Tier 3 intervention services may differ from Tier 1 services regarding the number of days per week and the amount of time per day that the supplemental Tier 2 and Tier 3 intervention services are provided to students. For instance, one response-to-intervention framework may call for Tier 2 services to be provided two to three days per week for thirty minutes per session while another framework may call for these services to be provided four days per week for thirty to forty-five minutes per session. These parameters set the stage for the real focus of Tier 2 and Tier 3 intervention services regarding time management, which is ensuring that students spend every available moment attending to the instruction that is presented and working on instructional level tasks.

In other words, the focus is on engaged and academic learning time, and the way that Tier 2 and Tier 3 intervention services are constructed and presented should result in these terms becoming nearly synonymous. Among other things, this might mean that the length of each Tier 2 or Tier 3 session may be shortened from the thirty to forty-five minutes that are called for because the students are not able to sustain their attention that long—particularly if the students' inability to sustain attention is a factor that is impeding their attainment of expected learning outcomes. Finally, it is important to note that, in the majority of instances when a student is provided Tier 2 or Tier 3 services, he also will continue to receive Tier 1 services.

One final point about the time that is available for the presentation of instruction and about which school personnel should remain mindful is the percentage of time during a student's life, from kindergarten through grade 12, that a student spends in school. If a school day is seven hours long and one school year consists of 180 days, then a student with a record of perfect attendance during the thirteen years she attended school from kindergarten through grade 12 would have spent 14 percent of her life in school during this time.

This relatively limited percentage of time that is available for instruction is reduced by non-instructional activities such as lunch, recess, restroom breaks, pep rallies, and transitioning from one class to the next. Altogether this information highlights the need for teachers to exercise efficient instructional time management on behalf of every student so as not to deny them an opportunity to learn if they are willing to put forth the effort that is required to do so.

High-Quality Instruction: Universal Principles of Effective Teaching and Evidence-Based Practices Specific to Academic Disciplines.

The third component of high-quality instruction is the use of effective teaching practices. These practices result from a combination of (a) universal effective teaching practices and (b) evidence-based practices that are specific to a subject matter area, or academic discipline. The information presented below pertains to universal effective teaching practices. Chapter 3 presents information about effective, evidence-based teaching practices for subject matter areas.

Relationship between universal effective teaching practices and evidence-based practices

Researchers have identified teacher behaviors that are directly related to the presentation of effective, high-quality instruction irrespective of the subject matter area that is the focus of instruction. For instance, an elementary school general education teacher who strives to present effective reading, math, science, and social studies lessons to the same group of students would demonstrate these behaviors in each lesson. Similarly, an Algebra 1 teacher would demonstrate these behaviors regardless of the topic she addresses, whether it be linear, quadratic, or exponential functions, or adding or factoring polynomials.

These universal practices are evidence-based and allow for the incorporation of scientifically-based instruction—also known as evidence-based practices—that are specific to a subject matter area, such as teaching beginning reading or math. The practices that are specific to a subject matter area often exclusively address the specific skills that need to be taught (e.g., in beginning reading instruction, both phonemic awareness and phonics), the sequence to follow to teach them (e.g., when teaching students letter names teach the names for letters whose shapes are quite dissimilar, such as f and s, before teaching the names for letters whose shapes are quite similar, such as m and n), and the types of instructional strategies that should be used (e.g., when teaching students phonemic awareness or phonics have the students look into a handheld mirror to see the positions of their tongue, teeth, and lips as they make different speech sounds).

Often, however, in research reports, the explanations of subject matter, evidence-based practices do not address some of the more intricate, and important, aspects of effective instruction. These include the topics addressed above (such as the features of an appropriate environmental arrangement or effective time management), as well as the use of universal effective teaching practices.

All of these practices, plus evidence-based practices specific to an academic discipline, combine to result in the presentation of high-quality instruction in a general education classroom. The challenge for teachers is how to interconnect them in a lesson.

Universal effective teaching practices

Universal effective teaching practices mostly refer to behaviors a teacher exhibits during a lesson rather than either what a teacher does (a) to set the stage for a lesson (e.g., create an appropriate environmental arrangement) or (b) after a lesson (e.g., evaluate assessment data to inform her instruction). A teacher who engages in universal effective teaching practices:

1. Presents a directive to students that indicates that a lesson is about to begin and requires them to respond in a way that indicates they are ready to attend to the instruction
2. Clearly states the lesson's learning objectives
3. Ties new content to what the students already know about the lesson's topic
4. Presents material in appropriate chunks, or small enough steps, that are sequenced to enhance clarity and minimize confusion
5. Solicits regular, active students responding in multiple ways (e.g., response cards, choral responding)
6. Monitors students' understanding, provides behavior-specific feedback rather than general statements of praise, and re-teaches as necessary—using something other than "more of the same"
7. Maintains a "laser-like," seamless focus on the lesson, not allowing herself or her students to disrupt the lesson (either through off-topic comments or questions, or other behaviors)
8. Employs visual supports (e.g., outlines, graphic organizers, study guides, task organizers) that serve multiple purposes, such as highlighting key ideas, pointing out the structure and flow of the content, depicting the strategies for solving a problem or completing a task while keeping track of the steps involved, or enabling students to retain in their short-term memory what the teacher just said
9. Conducts a review at, or near the end, of a lesson, in which the main points and integrative concepts are re-stated and previews the next, related lesson she will teach
10. Requires the completion of follow-up assignments that enable students to practice a skill or encode the material in the student's own words[8]

High-Quality Instruction: Focus on Core Curriculum Content

A fourth component of high-quality instruction is a clear focus on the content, or curriculum that is to be taught. As a practical matter it is unrealistic to assume that a student will attain expected outcomes if he is not taught the knowledge and skills that comprise the school's curriculum, and that are the basis for assessing a student's attainment of these outcomes. The term curriculum-assessment alignment refers to ensuring that the content that is taught is the content that is assessed.

Hence, two topics are addressed in the remainder of this section. One topic is the definition for, and development of, a curriculum. The second topic is the need to teach, in Tier 1, a curriculum that consists of both academic and school social behaviors. As was noted previously, historically an academic-oriented response-to-intervention framework has been associated with teaching reading. However, over time a linkage has been made between teaching students' academic skills and school social behaviors, particularly at Tier 1 of any multi-tier intervention framework.

Curriculum defined

In this book, the term curriculum refers solely to a listing of the knowledge and skills that students are to learn. Related, but separate, terms include (a) instructional strategies, which are the planned actions a teacher executes when she presents a lesson, (b) instructional materials, which refer to both the tangible (e.g., base ten blocks) and intangible (e.g., apps) items that are used during a lesson, and (c) assessments, which refer to the various means of collecting data that are then used to make decisions about past and future instruction. Some definitions for curriculum incorporate each of these terms. This, however, is not the case here.

Development: Who creates a curriculum and the ethics of teaching it

To highlight the saliency of the curriculum, it is important to note how and why it is developed. Quite often large and diverse groups of stakeholders, including educators, parents, politicians, and business leaders, work to establish a school's curriculum. Together they attempt to identify what they believe students should learn in grades K-12 so that they will be prepared for further education, employment, and living independently during their post-secondary years.

In other words, they identify the knowledge and skills that they believe are critically important for students to learn to be able to live interdependently as contributing members of a society. Consequently, some believe it is unethical to disregard teaching students their school's curriculum, and research has confirmed that "what gets taught is what gets learned."

Relationship between curriculum and universal effective teaching practices

In an RTI framework, high quality instruction is predicated on "teaching the right things." Therefore, the statement, "What gets taught is what gets learned," applies. Ultimately the framework's focus is "what gets learned" and is referred to as students' attainment of expected learning outcomes. These outcomes should be delineated in the curriculum.

The term *curriculum-assessment alignment* refers to the process of ensuring that the assessment items, whatever they are, are directly related to the content that is listed in a curriculum. Hence, the data that are obtained from the assessment component of the framework will reflect the students' mastery of the curriculum. Simply stated, it is unreasonable to expect a student to perform well on an assessment that is aligned with a curriculum that has not been taught.

A relevant issue that must be addressed is the refrain that "teachers are just teaching to the test." When the skills that are being taught are the skills that will be assessed for the purpose of determining whether students have attained expected levels and rates of achievement, and are the skills valued by the stakeholders who created the curriculum, then a teacher would be teaching to the test. The issue is, perhaps, a matter of degree (i.e., how often and in what manner does the teacher refer to the relationship between the curriculum and the assessment).

Teachers do need to teach their students strategies for taking assessments. Teachers need to make their students aware of how assessments are constructed so that the student's performance is a valid representation of his mastery of curriculum content rather than his test-taking abilities. Teaching these test-taking skills comprise what has been referred to as the hidden curriculum.

Curriculum focus is related to several universal effective teaching practices. Effective teachers promote student focus and active engagement. Furthermore, these teachers avoid diversions that alter this focus. This means that a teacher must be diligent in her efforts to focus both her and her students' work on the content that comprises the curriculum.

A student will not master math skills if, during the time that has been allocated to teach these skills, the student is engaged in activities that may divert his attention from learning the skills that are the focus of instruction. This could occur if a student engages with computer games that purport to teach math skills but instead result in the student focusing most of his attention on how to play the game rather than learn the skills (e.g., the student focuses more of his attention on how to increase his race car's speed, which is a critical feature of the game that is used to teach basic addition facts).

Critical academic discipline skills must be targeted

In some academic disciplines, research has identified the knowledge and skills that students must master to be proficient in the subject matter area. One component of high-quality instruction in these disciplines would be teaching a curriculum that consisted of this content.

For example, a review of the scientific research[9] identified what are referred to as the five big ideas of reading instruction: phonemic awareness, phonics, vocabulary, fluency, and reading comprehension. Students need to master the curriculum across these five areas to become proficient, independent, skilled readers. High-quality reading instruction in general education classrooms would focus on teaching these skills.

Furthermore, research has identified the sequence, or order, in which certain skills are to be taught. One reason for this arrangement is that the mastery of more advanced, higher order skills depends upon the mastery of more basic, fundamental, lower order skills. An example is teaching addition before multiplication since one way of thinking about multiplication is as repeated addition. Likewise, skills that lead to successful beginning reading performance must be taught and mastered in order for a student to be able to use reading as a means to acquire information from print at higher grade levels across academic disciplines. These considerations are another element of an appropriate curriculum focus.

A second reason for this arrangement is that listing the content that is to be taught (i.e., the scope of the curriculum) and the sequence (i.e., the order) will contribute to the establishment of the rate, or pace, at which it is to be taught. These standards—particularly the rate at which students are expected to master skills—will determine which students are at risk for failure and, therefore, need to be provided Tier 2 or Tier 3 intervention services. For instance, students who are designated as being either (a) at-risk for failure or (b) eligible to receive special education services are not demonstrating the attainment of targeted learning outcomes in the core curriculum that are at an expected level or rate.

While the core curriculum should consist of clear statements of the skills students are to master, high-quality instruction will result in students learning connections among the skills as well (i.e., big ideas), and strategies for when and how to apply the "individual elements in a network of related content" because doing so demonstrates mastery of the subject matter area instruction. For example, students learn to use phonics skills for the purpose of identifying an unknown word, and then use context clues, or prior experience with the word, to determine its meaning, as well as the meaning of the passage being read.

Likewise, students apply basic math skills in the context of comparing linear equations which represent the costs associated with certain apartment rental plans to determine which plan is best for their budget. The three "C's"—comprehensive, clear, and cohesive—should be evident in the teaching of the curriculum in a general education classroom in which high-quality instruction is presented.

Importance of academic learning time

A general education classroom in which high-quality instruction is presented will focus its work on the skills that comprise the core curriculum and will do so in a way that affords students maximum academic learning time. Students need to be taught skills that are at their instructional level rather than skills that are significantly beneath or above this level. The latter circumstance may result from a school policy that requires teachers to present prescribed content according to a pacing guide, which results in prescribed curriculum content being taught on a designated day and at a designated time irrespective if this is the content a student should be taught in accordance with their instructional level.

Use of a pacing guide as just described will increase the probability that a student will engage in off-task behavior. Students need to be challenged appropriately so that they expend their efforts engaged in on-task, instructionally relevant behaviors rather than engaged in disruptive behaviors, because they are either bored with tasks that they perceive to be too easy or are frustrated and overwhelmed with tasks that they perceive to be too difficult.

Reasons for addressing both academic and school social behaviors in Tier 1 of an RTI framework

In spite of research that has documented the direct relationships that exist between both teaching and learning academic and school social behaviors, some teachers do not believe they should have to spend time teaching students' social behaviors nor see a reason for doing so. Rather, these teachers see their role as applying consequences to displays of inappropriate behavior. Historically teachers have applied consequences intended to function as punishment. These consequences include reprimands, loss of privileges, office referrals, after school detention, suspension, and expulsion.

Many teachers who do not believe that they should have to spend time teaching school social behaviors contend that their job is to teach students academic skills. Their position is supported by the fact that the vast majority of core curriculum state standards address academic skills exclusively.

Furthermore, some teachers who do not see a reason for having to teach students school social behaviors believe that students are capable of figuring out, on their own, how to behave appropriately. That is to say, these teachers believe that students can intuit how to behave appropriately simply by observing others do so. Additionally, these teachers surmise that other adults, such as a child's parents, are responsible for teaching their child how to behave appropriately while at school.

When appropriate school social behaviors are conceptualized as the behaviors that students are to display for the purpose of sharing both their classroom and non-classroom school space safely with others and in a manner that allows for the efficient presentation of effective instruction, then teachers can readily identify many of these behaviors that they, in fact, do teach.

Still, a number of teachers need to be made cognizant of some of the reasons why they need to either directly teach students appropriate school social behaviors or steps they can take that will increase the probability that students will engage in these behaviors.[10,11]

1. Appropriate social behavior is context specific. This means that there is no such thing as generic, appropriate school social behavior. For example, in some schools, students are permitted to use their cell phones in accordance with certain guidelines while in other schools all cell phone use is strictly prohibited.

   Often times local norms, as referenced above regarding who develops a curriculum rather than research result in the identification of the social behaviors to teach. With respect to teaching students how to engage in appropriate school social behaviors, aside from matters that readily pertain to safe schools (i.e., bring only books not weapons), appropriate school social behaviors will be context specific and, therefore, locally defined.

2. A more efficient use of a teacher's time is to explicitly teach students the social behaviors that are appropriate in their school than is operating under the assumption that students know which behaviors are appropriate and how to engage in them, and for teachers to only address students' engagement in inappropriate behaviors when students disrupt class by engaging in these behaviors. Teaching appropriate school social behavior, such as how to transition efficiently across activities, can maximize a teacher's use of her allocated time.

3. Many students with disabilities will be in general education classes and the individualized education plans (IEPs) for some of these students will require their general educations teachers to provide instruction about appropriate school social behaviors.

4. The presentation of inappropriate academic instruction can set the stage for a student's display of inappropriate school social behavior. This means that inappropriate academic instruction can function as an antecedent for a student's engagement in inappropriate social behavior. A student who becomes frustrated because he cannot complete academic tasks that far exceed his current instructional level is more likely to engage in inappropriate social behavior than is a student who remains engaged in assigned tasks that are challenging but target the student's instructional needs.

RTI Tier 1 curriculum focus: From academics only to instruction about academics plus school social behavior

Previously it was noted that multi-tier intervention systems were initially created with different focal points. The first response-to-intervention frameworks addressed what would be considered the teaching of traditional academic content, such as reading and math skills. In fact, initially an academically-oriented response-to-intervention framework was very closely associated with beginning reading instruction.

Another multi-tier intervention system, Positive Behavior Interventions and Supports (PBIS), was developed to address teaching students how to behave appropriately at school. In this book, the term school social behavior is used to refer to these types of behaviors.

Nevertheless, even though different frameworks have been created to address different skills, the frameworks are related in several ways. First, they are comprised of a tiered intervention component that involves providing additional services, beyond those provided in the general education classroom, to a relatively small number of students who still have not attained expected learning outcomes. Second, the frameworks are related by the fact that research has confirmed the linkage that exists between the teaching of academic skills and school social behaviors.

As a number of educators have noted it is difficult to pinpoint where the teaching of academic skills ends, and school social behaviors begins—or vice versa. Moreover, an estimated one-third of students fail to learn because of psychosocial problems that interfere with their ability to fully attend to and engage in instructional activities.

Third, broadly speaking, each framework addresses students' behaviors. Behavior can be defined as one's observable actions, meaning anything a person says or does. Given this definition of behavior and the established linkage between academic and social behaviors, one would be hard pressed to justify saying—which some professionals have done—that they cannot teach one type of behavior (academic skills) until they have effectively taught a child how to consistently display another type of behavior (appropriate social behaviors). Specifically, some educators have asserted that they "cannot teach academics until they have a student's behaviors under control."

Since the purpose of this book is to provide you with a fundamental understanding of the framework, the linkage between academic and social behavior is highlighted and addressed within the context of high-quality Tier 1 intervention services. Subsequently the discussions about Tier 2 and Tier 3 intervention services are mostly based upon a consideration of academic skills instruction. Yet, you must not lose sight of the fact that students' engagement in appropriate school social behavior is equally important when they are being provided Tier 2 and Tier 3 services.

Finally, other terms, such as Multi-Tier Systems of Support (MTSS), have been coined to refer to the use of one of the two original multi-tier intervention frameworks or a hybrid framework that ties both together. Yet, the term "response-to-intervention" framework is used in this book for a number of reasons that were explained previously, including the facts that (a) the underlying operational feature of any multi-tier intervention framework is to assess how a student responds to the intervention services provided so that these services are either continued or adjusted as necessary, (b) nearly every state references the response-to-intervention framework in its policies, and (c) the majority of school districts reportedly have at least one school that uses response-to-intervention. Consequently, it is a multi-tier intervention framework term with which most people are familiar.

Curriculum focus: Functional performance versus academic achievement

Since a response-to-intervention framework accounts for every student's performance, it is necessary to note how the curriculum for some students with disabilities will differ from their same-age peers' curriculum. These students will receive Tier 3 intervention services, so this topic will be addressed again in chapter 5. For now, it is important to note that some students with disabilities will be expected to master skills that have been set forth in their IEPs but are far removed from the curriculum that has been designated to be taught in the general education classroom.

High-Quality Instruction: Valid, Reliable Assessment

The last component of high-quality instruction is valid, reliable assessment. Specifically, this is the use of data from assessments that informs instruction. These data are meaningful to the extent that the assessments are aligned with the curriculum and the curriculum has been taught.

The assessment component of an RTI framework consists of screening and ongoing progress monitoring. In this framework screening refers to identifying the students who have a low probability of attaining expected learning outcomes due solely to receiving Tier 1 services. Progress monitoring assessments produce data regarding students' level and rate of progress. These assessments are (a) aligned with the curriculum that is taught, (b) provide information about students' attainment of expected learning outcomes, and (c) result in data that informs instruction. This means the data provide the teacher with information that is useful in adjusting instruction.

Progress monitoring contributes to high-quality instruction because it allows a teacher to make data-based decisions concerning both what to teach and how to present instruction. These data increase the probability that a teacher will address content that is at a student's instructional level. The data also may indicate which component of high-quality instruction needs to be modified so that it is effective. This is an important reason why high-quality instruction needs to be operationally defined. Chapter 6 addresses the topic of assessment and its place in the framework in detail.

CHAPTER 2 COMPREHENSION CHECK

Now that you have finished reading the chapter, you should be able to:

- State the type of instruction that should be presented in a general education classroom where Tier 1 services are being provided.
- Explain what is meant by an "operational definition."
- Discuss one problem with defining high-quality instruction only in terms of student outcomes.
- Define the terms "effective instruction" and "learning objective."
- Operationally define high-quality instruction in terms of (a) environmental arrangements, (b) time management, (c) universal and discipline-specific effective instructional strategies, (d) curriculum, and (e) assessment.
- Define the term curriculum.
- Explain what is meant by a curriculum's scope and sequence.
- Define the term "accommodation" and list one example.
- Differentiate between academics and school social behaviors.

NOTES

1. Michael Epstein, Marc Atkins, Douglas Cullinan, Krista Kutash, and K. Weaver, "Reducing Behavior Problems in the Elementary School Classroom," *IES Practice Guide* 20, no. 8 (2008): 12–22.

2. Bob Algozzine, R. Putman, and R. H. Horner, "Support for Teaching Students with Learning Disabilities Academic Skills and Social Behaviors within a Response-to-Intervention

Model: Why It Doesn't Matter What Comes First," *Insights on Learning Disabilities* 9, no. 1 (2012): 7–36.

3. Bob Algozzine, Chuang Wang, Richard White, Nancy Cooke, Mary Beth Marr, Kate Algozzine, Shawnna S. Helf, and Grace Zamora Duran, "Effects of Multi-Tier Academic and Behavior Instruction on Difficult-to-Teach Students," *Exceptional Children* 79, no. 1 (2012): 45–64.

4. Michael Epstein, Marc Atkins, Douglas Cullinan, Krista Kutash, and K. Weaver, "Reducing Behavior Problems in the Elementary School Classroom," *IES Practice Guide* 20, no. 8 (2008): 12–22.

5. R. H. Horner, G. Sugai, A. W. Todd, T. Lewis-Palmer, L. Bambara, and L. Kern, *Individualized Supports for Students with Problem Behaviors: Designing Positive Behavior Plans*, (2005).

6. John W. Maag, *Behavior Management: From Theoretical Implications to Practical Applications*, 2nd edition, Belmont, CA: Edith Beard Brady, 2004.

7. Michael S. Rosenberg, Lawrence J. O'Shea, and Dorothy J. O'Shea, *Student Teacher to Master Teacher: A Practical Guide for Educating Students with Special Needs* (Prentice Hall, 2001).

8. Jere E. Brophy, *Teaching*, International Academy of Education and the International Bureau of Education. 1999. Available at www.cklavya.org/edu-practices_01_eng.pdf.

9. National Reading Panel (US), National Institute of Child Health, and Human Development (US), *Teaching Children to Read: An Evidence-Based Assessment of the Scientific Research Literature on Reading and Its Implications for Reading Instruction* (National Institute of Child Health and Human Development, National Institutes of Health, 2000). Available at http://www.nationalreadingpanel.org/Publications/summary.htm.

10. Lee Kern and Nathan H. Clemens, "Antecedent Strategies to Promote Appropriate Classroom Behavior," *Psychology in the Schools* 44, no. 1 (2007): 65–75.

11. H. M. Walker, E. Ramsey, and F. M. Gresham, "Antisocial Behavior in School: Evidence-Based Practices," (Belmont, CA: Wadswoth/Thomson Learning, 2004).

Chapter Three

Tier 1 and
Scientifically Based Instruction

OVERVIEW

In this chapter you will learn about scientifically based instruction and how it relates to Tier 1 services in an RTI framework. Key points from the chapter include the following:

Scientifically based instruction is a key element of a response-to-intervention framework's Tier 1 services.

The term *evidence-base practice* (EBP) is now more commonly used in place of scientifically based instruction. EBPs refer to interventions whose effectiveness are supported by multiple research studies.

Scientific research, via the use of the scientific method, attempts to discover relationships between phenomena in the environment. In experimental educational research, an attempt is made to discover the relationship between an instructional strategy and students' behaviors.

Only experimental research designs address whether the independent variable (e.g., an instructional strategy) causes a change in the dependent variable (e.g., the attainment, by a student, of one or more targeted learning outcomes).

Three types of experimental educational research include group experimental studies, quasi-group experimental studies, and single-subject experimental studies.

An EBP refers to an intervention that has been the focus of multiple research studies. An EBP is identified by way of an evidence-based review, which involves an evaluation of the research across a number of relevant dimensions, such as the integrity of the research design and its magnitude of effect.

One example of Tier 1 high-quality, scientifically based instruction is K-2 beginning reading instruction that addresses key curriculum content (e.g., phonics and vocabulary) that is taught through explicit instruction that is presented in an orderly classroom.

SCIENTIFICALLY BASED INSTRUCTION
AND EVIDENCE-BASED PRACTICES

As was noted at the outset of chapter 2, Tier 1 services are, generally speaking, the same in any response-to-intervention framework regardless of the total number of tiers that comprise the framework. Specifically, Tier 1 consists of the presentation of what is referred to as high quality, scientifically based instruction in the general education classroom. Chapter 2 focused almost exclusively on the details of high-quality instruction, but did reference its relationship to scientifically based instruction, which is the focus of this chapter.

Chapter 2 noted a linkage between high-quality instruction and scientifically based instruction in a way that could lead one to conclude that the use of scientifically based instruction, in and of itself, resulted in the presentation of high-quality instruction. However, chapter 2 explained how high-quality instruction is actually comprised of a number of components, which include universal effective teaching practices in conjunction with scientifically based instruction that pertains to an academic discipline.

In addition to the term scientifically based instruction, a wide variety of terms have been used, synonymously, in the professional literature. These terms include scientific research-based instruction, research-based procedures, research-based instruction, evidence-based intervention, and peer-reviewed research. In this book another synonymous term, evidence-based practice, is used. It is explained in this chapter and then used throughout the remainder of the book since it is now more commonly used than are the other terms.

At the end of this chapter an explanation of how multiple types of evidence-based practices can be presented simultaneously for the purpose of providing students with high-quality, Tier 1 beginning reading instruction in an RTI framework is offered as an example of the application of scientifically based instruction as one component of high-quality instruction.

GENESIS OF EVIDENCE BASED PRACTICES

Work on identifying evidence-based practices resulted from research that reported many teachers did not routinely implement interventions that were shown by reliable research to result in students' attainment of expected learning outcomes. Instead teachers relied on matters such as expert opinion, personal experiences, and tradition to settle upon interventions.[1] In response to this circumstance legislation was passed that required teachers to present instruction that was based upon scientific-based research as opposed to popular current trends not supported by research.[2] In other words, decisions about instruction were to be based on objective data more so than subjective information.

Both the No Child Left Behind Act and the Individuals with Disabilities Education Act used various terms (see above) to refer to the sources of objective data that educators were to rely upon. Regardless the term used, the intent was to base instruction on data obtained from research that employed the scientific method. Specifically, the No Child Left Behind Act noted that scientific research is comprised of objective, rigorous, and replicable procedures that are used to obtain reliable and valid knowledge about educational activities.[3]

In professional literature, the term evidence-based practices came to be used to refer to educational activities that have research documenting their effectiveness.[4] Moreover, the term meant that multiple, reputable studies of these activities have produced consistent results. The term makes clear that the weight of the evidence, rather than a single study, establishes an instructional strategy to be effective. The difficulty in using the term lies in agreeing upon how to determine, or establish, the weight of this evidence. Among the questions that must be answered are how many studies must be conducted, what type of research design produces these data, and how will this research to be evaluated to ensure that it was conducted properly, or is of sufficient quality?

These topics are addressed below. First, the scientific method and its use in educational research is discussed. Afterwards, the process that is followed to identify evidence-based practices is explained.

THE SCIENTIFIC METHOD AND SCIENTIFICALLY BASED INSTRUCTION

Scientific research attempts to discover relationships between phenomena in the environment. These relationships are discovered through experiments. In an experiment a researcher is attempting to discover a functional, or causal, relationship between what are called the independent and dependent variable. That is to say, does the independent variable (e.g., an instructional strategy) *cause* a change in the dependent variable (e.g., the attainment, by a student, of one or more targeted outcomes).

The scientific method refers to the steps researchers follow to conduct an experiment that serves as the basis for scientific inquiry or research. While the method can vary across researchers, generally it consists of the steps discussed here.

First, a researcher needs to develop a hypothesis, which is a statement (referred to as an educated guess) about the causal relationship she believes exists between an independent and dependent variable. One way a researcher can accomplish this is by exploring her topic of interest through engaging in activities such as reading relevant articles in professional journals and speaking with colleagues.

When a researcher develops her hypothesis, she will define both the independent and dependent variables in observable and measurable terms. Once this is accomplished, she conducts an experiment to determine whether the independent variable influences, meaning changes in some way, the dependent variable. To ensure that she can attribute changes in the dependent variable to the independent variable, she must control all other variables that might be explained as the reason for any changes she documents. Control means to keep these variables constant or not allow them to change in a way that can explain any changes that occur in the experiment.

In educational research, independent variables are often the instructional strategies teachers employ while dependent variables are the expected learning outcomes we want students to attain (e.g., the academic and school social behaviors we want them to acquire). An example of an experiment in educational research might consist of the researcher identifying a student's academic behavior that she wants to change, such as the student being able to read high frequency words.

The researcher might decide to focus on this skill because (a) she has noted, through her observations in schools, discussions with colleagues, and reading scholarly articles, that a noteworthy number of students have not attained the skill despite receiving instruction from commercial reading programs that are in widespread use, and that (b) mastery of the skill is essential for the student to become a proficient reader. Thus, the researcher would seek to identify an instructional strategy that would be effective in teaching students the skill of reading high frequency words. An example of a how a relevant experiment that pertains to teaching a student with disability how to read high frequency words would evolve is as follows.

After gathering an extensive amount of information about her topic of interest (e.g., by observing lessons and reading research about teaching students with disabilities how to read high frequency words), a researcher concludes that in order to learn how to read high frequency words, the student needs to increase his time on task, number of opportunities to respond during a lesson and his receipt of differential feedback. She then posits a hypothesis that if a teacher employs an instructional strategy that is comprised of these elements, the student will learn how to read the high frequency words that have been targeted for his mastery.

In this experiment the instructional strategy would be the independent variable while the targeted student outcome—the student learning to read previously unknown high frequency words—would be the dependent variable since it depends upon the influence or effectiveness of the independent variable.

It is important to remain cognizant of the fact that desired student outcomes might involve decreasing an inappropriate behavior rather than increasing a desired behavior. An example of an inappropriate behavior that may need to be decreased would be a student asking an excessive number of questions about how to put away art supplies after being told to do so. An independent variable that may prove, through an experiment, to be effective in decreasing this behavior would consist of a visual support which depicted the steps a student is to follow to put away art supplies. Thus, this experiment could be designed and conducted to improve a student outcome by both decreasing an inappropriate behavior (i.e., asking excessive questions) while simultaneously increasing an appropriate behavior (i.e., independently putting away art supplies).

These are just two, relatively simple explanations of experiments that address educational interventions and that could be characterized as scientifically based. There are many different protocols, called research designs, which are used to find answers to the numerous questions that need to be answered to determine what teachers need to do to produce desired student learning outcomes. Furthermore, as was noted previously, no one study is viewed as providing the definitive answer to any proposed hypothesis. Rather, the accumulation of similar findings across multiple replications of experiments lead to a conclusion about how things work.

Objective measures and the weight of the evidence are central to the identification of an evidence-based practice. In part, an evidence-based practice is identified through the examination of the research designs that were used to produce the evidence in support of it. The following discussion explains several of the different types of experimental educational research designs that result in the identification of effective, evidence-based instructional strategies.

EXPERIMENTAL EDUCATIONAL RESEARCH

There are numerous ways to conduct research, and the way a study is conducted is referred to as its research design. It is important for you to understand that different research designs produce information that can be used to answer certain questions but not others.

For instance, if a researcher wanted to learn about teachers' feelings toward an instructional strategy, to include why they did or did not continue using it after a designated period of time, the researcher would use a qualitative research design. The knowledge this researcher gained, however, could not be used to determine if the instructional strategy was effective. To determine the effectiveness of an instructional strategy a researcher would have to use an experimental research design.

This design seeks to determine if there is a causal relationship between an intervention and a desired student outcome. This is the type of design that results in the scientifically based instruction that is at the heart of Tier 1 services in a response-to-intervention framework. Three general types of experimental research designs are group experimental studies, quasi-group experimental studies, and single-subject studies.

In a group experimental study, the researcher would compare the outcomes of students who had been systematically assigned to two groups—an experimental group and a control group—such that the groups were considered to be similar in all key respects at the outcome of the study. The researcher would systematically implement the intervention being studied with the students in the experimental group. The students in the control group would not receive the intervention, which would be the only variable that differed between the two groups. If the experimental group realized noteworthy, better outcomes than the control group, the researcher would conclude that the intervention was the reason for, or cause of, the outcome.

In a quasi-group experimental study, the researcher would use pre-existing groups rather than randomly assigning participants to groups. The researcher would systematically implement the intervention being studied with the students in the experimental group, whereas the students in the control group would not receive the intervention and would continue with what is referred to as "business as usual."

However, the non-random assignment of participants to the two groups may mean that they vary in relevant ways (e.g., ability levels; their teacher's experience; or, how the focus of the study, such as teaching reading, was taught in previous years) that may be plausible explanations for the reason why different outcomes were realized between groups, rather than just the independent variable being the plausible explanation.

In a single-subject experimental study, a researcher would repeatedly apply the intervention to one student, who would serve as his own control. The control, or baseline, condition would reflect the student's performance with respect to the dependent variable without only the independent variable.

Next, the intervention, or independent variable, would be applied in what is called the experimental condition. If both a change in the level and trend of the student's performance data were observed, the researcher would conclude that the intervention was effective since it caused what is called a robust change in the student's behavior. The researcher would have to demonstrate this change several or more times to increase her confidence in explaining the functional relationship between the independent and dependent variables.[5]

IDENTIFYING EVIDENCE-BASED PRACTICES

An evidence-based practice refers to an intervention that has been the focus of multiple research studies and, in these studies, has been shown to be effective with respect to students' attainment of targeted learning outcomes.[6] Hence, the identification of an evidence-based practice involves a labor intensive, multi-step process[7] that is called an evidence-based review.[8,9,10,11] While the specific steps that are followed in each review may differ, generally speaking each review involves the execution of the following steps:

a. The identification of the topic that is the focus of the research studies that are being evaluated. The topic is the intervention, or instructional strategy, that is, the focus of the research.
b. The location where the research was published. Nowadays, there are many locations where a research study can be published, including scholarly journals, textbooks, and on the internet. The research that lends most credibility to an evidence-based intervention is published in what are called peer-reviewed journals, which are publications that require several colleagues to evaluate the worthiness of the research.
c. Listing, as well as defining, of the features of the research that will be evaluated. A number of these features are identified and explained below.
d. The assignment of a score—or rating—for each feature, as well as the study as a whole, and
e. a determination of how the overall score will be evaluated. In general, studies that have a higher overall score are considered to present the most valid evidence in support of an intervention's effectiveness. Further, the designation of an evidence-based practice occurs when an intervention has been validated via multiple studies with high overall scores.

Typically, during an evidence-based review four features of the studies that have been identified for the review are evaluated. For each study, three features are evaluated: research design, quality, and magnitude of effect. The fourth feature that is evaluated in an evidence-based review is the quantity of research. All of these features are explained below:

Research design

A research design refers to the methods or procedures that are used to conduct a study, such as how data will be collected and analyzed. As was noted previously, there are many research designs and these designs can be used to answer some types of research questions but not others.

Only experimental research designs address whether the independent variable (e.g., an instructional strategy) *causes* a change in the dependent variable (e.g., the attainment, by a student, of one or more targeted learning outcomes). Other research designs provide results that inform instruction (e.g., whether teachers prefer to use one approach to schoolwide positive behavior support over another) but do not answer questions about the effectiveness of instructional strategies that are directly related to student outcomes.[12]

Quality of research studies

This refers to the extent to which a study was conducted in accordance with its prescribed research design. For example, an experimental study would be examined to determine if data were collected to verify that the independent variable was implemented as it was supposed to be, and that the dependent variable was measured as intended.

Magnitude of effect

Magnitude of effect refers to the amount of change in the dependent variable that is realized from the implementation of the independent variable. An effective instructional strategy should produce noteworthy impact on student learning outcomes and be both statistically and educationally significant.

Regarding student learning outcomes, if an intervention was designed to enable a student to attain an academic skill or a school social behavior, then the student's performance data should clearly reflect these results. Likewise—but conversely—if an intervention was designed to reduce or eliminate the student's performance of an inappropriate school social behavior, one that interferes with the student's learning and that of his peers (i.e., loudly and routinely blurting comments that do not contribute to the teacher's instruction), the performance data should clearly reflect these results as well.

The term *statistical significance* refers to instances when the data from a study show one of the results that were explained in the previous paragraph, and that these data can be attributed to an identifiable cause. In experimental research designs, the independent variable is the identifiable cause. As was noted previously, a question worth asking is whether statistically significant results are also educationally significant.

Educational significance

Educational significance refers to how readily the results of a study can be applied in a typical school setting. For example, the data from a study might be statistically significant with regard to showing that the use of a uniquely designed $15,000 computer program was effective in teaching one student how to add mixed numerals. Yet, the educational significance of these results would be completely meaningless to most teachers since they would not be able to spend $15,000 to teach a single student a single math skill.

Quantity of research

An initial, one-time-only study that indicates an intervention was effective is not sufficient evidence for characterizing an instructional strategy as being an evidence-based practice. Rather, the question that needs to be answered in the affirmative is, "Do the results from multiple credible studies support their effectiveness?" Each evidence-based review sets its own criteria regarding the quantity of research that must exist for an intervention to be identified as an evidence-based practice.

As was noted previously a score, or rating, is assigned for each feature. Then, based on some type of summary of these scores, an overall grade is assigned to the intervention that is the focus of the evidence-based review. The final grade assigned to the intervention determines whether it is designated to be an evidence-based practice. In other words, to be designated as an evidence-based practice the intervention has to receive what has been determined to be a passing grade by those who set out to conduct the evidence-based review.

Understandably, different criteria for evaluating research and assigning scores have been used across different evidence-based reviews. This has resulted in an intervention being identified as having sufficient evidence to be characterized as an evidence-based practice in one instance but not in another.

This outcome certainly poses challenges for practitioners who, in accordance with a response-to-intervention framework, are expected to present high-quality instruction in the general education classroom that is based, in large part, upon the information presented through evidence-based reviews. A related challenge for practitioners is staying abreast of the most recently published work in this regard and, in the case of general education teachers who teach multiple subjects, doing so across multiple academic disciplines.

It is important to remain mindful of the fact that evidence-based reviews of interventions are to be used as guides in the sense that these reviews function as starting points in the decision-making process that is followed for deciding how to intervene with a student.[13,14] In a response-to-intervention framework, this decision-making process subsequently will also include the consideration of ongoing progress monitoring data. Altogether teachers will use multiple types of information when they exercise their professional judgements regarding how to present effective instruction. [15,16,17,18]

TIER 2 AND 3 INTERVENTION SERVICES
AND EVIDENCE BASED PRACTICES

Until now the discussion has centered on Tier 1 intervention services to further examine what is meant by both high-quality instruction and scientifically based instruction. However, it is just as important for Tier 2 and Tier 3 intervention services to also be predicated on evidence-based practices even though, in much of the relevant literature, not as much emphasis has been placed on these practices and the presentation of high-quality, scientifically based instruction in these tiers. Rather, the emphasis has been placed on manipulating the intensity and nature of the instruction using small group arrangements.

BEGINNING READING INSTRUCTION:
HIGH-QUALITY AND SCIENTIFICALLY BASED

The information that is presented in this section is one example of how the features of high-quality instruction combine with evidence-based practices to result in the Tier 1 academic instruction that is called for in an RTI framework. Beginning reading instruction is the subject matter area that is addressed in this example.

First, a brief review of the features of high-quality instruction that were the focus of chapter 2 is presented. This review begins to reference the application of these features to beginning reading instruction. Afterward, several topics that pertain to the discipline of beginning reading instruction are addressed for the purposes of not only highlighting the fact that teaching students to read is a complex undertaking but also explain the work that has been performed to identify the curricula that needs to be taught.

Effective instructional strategies for teaching this curriculum are also cited. The example concludes with a somewhat detailed explanation of how the features of high-quality instruction combine with evidence-based practices specific to beginning reading instruction to result in the Tier 1 services that are called for in an RTI framework.

High-Quality Beginning Reading Instruction: A Blend of Universal Effective Teaching Practices and Evidence-Based Practices Specific to the Teaching of Reading

The extent to which students will become proficient readers will depend, in large part, upon their receipt of effective instruction. Effective, or high quality, beginning reading instruction will result from the interconnection of universal effective teaching practices and evidence-based practices that are more specific to the academic discipline of teaching beginning reading skills. In practical terms this means that high quality instruction must address the following universal and discipline-specific issues:

1. A safe, orderly setting in which the instruction is presented
2. A curriculum that consists of the discipline-specific knowledge and skills that research has identified as being necessary for attaining the instructional goal (As you will learn, this curriculum will consist of skills such as phonemic awareness and reading fluency.)
3. The use of effective, efficient, evidence-based practices that are a combination of universal effective teaching practices plus instructional strategies and materials that have been shown to be effective in teaching critical subject area skills which, in this case, are beginning reading skills
4. Appropriate time management
5. The use of an assessment protocol to measure the level and rate of student progress toward the learning goal (i.e., becoming a proficient reader), and that provides data to inform instruction

BEGINNING READING INSTRUCTION: TEACHING READING IS ROCKET SCIENCE

Teachers must teach students numerous skills across multiple grades to enable them to become proficient readers. Given factors such as the inherent complexity of the English language, students' biological makeup that is not naturally inclined to learn how to read, and the need to provide students with effective and coordinated instruction over a number of years, it is understandable why teaching students to become proficient readers has been characterized as a very complex task.[19,20] In fact, one noted author has compared a teacher's job of learning about, and subsequently presenting, effective reading instruction to the complexity associated with the discipline of rocket science.[21]

While the outcome of this instruction would be a student who is equipped with the knowledge and skills needed to both decipher and comprehend the written word (i.e., as a result of this instruction the student needs to be able to decode each word in a passage as well as determinc the meaning that is conveyed via the connected text), it begins with teaching skills that may not be readily identifiable as being central to the process of learning how to read but have proven to be via scientific research. This approach to beginning reading instruction is in keeping with some of the work that is performed at the outset of the use of a response-to-intervention framework. It is the identification of curricula that needs to be taught followed by the subsequent establishment of standards students must meet for the purpose of demonstrating their mastery of the curriculum.

ORIGIN OF EVIDENCE-BASED PRACTICES FOR READING INSTRUCTION, AND THE RTI FRAMEWORK

The first, or initial, response-to-intervention frameworks were developed to address the application of the knowledge that had accrued regarding evidence-based practices for teaching students how read. Three seminal publications included the book, *Beginning to Read: Thinking and Learning About Print*,[22] and two subsequent reports.[23,24] The three were based upon the authors' extensive reviews of scientific research.

Beginning to Read: Thinking and Learning About Print addressed two divergent, competing perspectives regarding the most appropriate way to teach students how to read: a whole language versus phonics-based approach. While the various processes involved in learning how to read were explained in-depth, a noteworthy conclusion was that effective beginning reading instruction needed to explicitly address phonics.

About a decade later, the two national reports referenced above supported this position. Both reports were based on an exhaustive review of the research. Altogether these publications put forth what have been described as the five big ideas of reading instruction: phonemic awareness, phonics, vocabulary, fluency, and reading comprehension. The significance behind the identification of these ideas is that students needed to be taught the knowledge and skills that comprise each idea in order to become proficient readers.

A point that was made repeatedly in the literature that addresses effective reading instruction was that students needed to attain sufficient reading proficiency standards by the end of third grade. Among other things this meant that teaching students how to read needed to be a primary focus of a school's curriculum during grades K-3. Subsequently, beginning in the fourth grade, the curriculum focus shifts to having students use their reading skills to acquire knowledge in content areas such as math, science, and social studies.

THE FIVE BIG IDEAS FROM
EVIDENCE-BASED READING RESEARCH

As was noted above, research that has addressed the content that needs to be taught to students to enable them to become proficient readers has identified by what have been referred to as the five big ideas of reading instruction.[25] These big ideas can be conceptualized as the five primary domains that encompass the knowledge and subskills students must master to become proficient readers. In turn, core curriculum standards are based on the content that comprise these domains. Each is discussed briefly below.

Phonological awareness

Phonological awareness refers to teaching students about the underlying sound structure of an oral language. It includes awareness of word parts, such as syllables, and individual speech sounds, referred to as phonemes.

Phonics

Phonics instruction involves teaching students the relationship between the phonemes that comprise an oral language and the graphemes, or letters of an alphabet, that stand for these phonemes (i.e., print). This connection is referred to as the alphabetic principle.

Fluency

Fluency refers to a student's reading rate, typically reported as the number of words read correctly per minute. One aspect of fluency is prosody, which encompasses the use of correct intonation that is based, in part, upon grammatical markers in print (e.g., using a rising voice when a sentence ends with a question mark or an emphatic voice when a sentence ends with an exclamation point).

Vocabulary

The words that comprise the English language are its vocabulary. Students must not only learn to read these words but also express their individual and multiple meanings.

Reading comprehension

Proficient readers need to demonstrate an understanding of what they have read. This is the ultimate goal of learning how to read. Comprehension consists of multiple elements which include, but are not limited to, a demonstration of an understanding of both the literal and inferential meanings conveyed in a passage.

In summary, it has been noted that effective beginning reading instruction incorporates use of the following evidence-based skills:[26,27,28,29,30,31,32,33,34,35]

1. Awareness of and ability to manipulate phonemes in segmenting and blending strategies
2. Awareness and understanding of letter-sound correspondence
3. The ability to translate the speech stream sound structures of oral language (phonological processing) into written language
4. Fluency in decoding words and understanding word meaning
5. The ability to demonstrate an understanding of what was read (e.g., retelling a passage; answering questions that are directly related to the content presented in a passage)

High-Quality, Evidence-Based Instructional Strategies for Presenting Tier 1 Beginning Reading Instruction

With respect to some of the evidence-based instructional strategies that are critical to teaching these skills,[36,37,38] it has been noted that instructional design for beginning reading instruction needs to be based on explicit instructional strategies (e.g., cognitive and direct instruction and behavioral strategies) using multiple exemplars and repeated practice.[39,40,41,42] To become proficient readers by the end of the third grade, children need many opportunities to apply these skills.[43,44,45]

HIGH-QUALITY READING INSTRUCTION: REVISITING A BLEND OF UNIVERSAL EFFECTIVE TEACHING PRACTICES AND EVIDENCE-BASED PRACTICES SPECIFIC TO THE TEACHING OF READING

Previously, a brief review of the features of high-quality instruction that were the focus of chapter 2 was presented and their application to beginning reading instruction was referenced. Below this topic is revisited in greater detail with the intent of providing one example of the interconnection between high-quality and evidence-based practices in Tier 1 in order to present effective beginning reading instruction:

The creation of a safe, orderly general education classroom that is set up and operated in accordance with established universal effective interventions. This includes: clear lines of sight (that would allow each student to see the teacher's face as she was pronouncing a phoneme as well as the letter of the alphabet she was showing while she was teaching a phonics lesson); limited distractions (particularly auditory distractions that might prevent some students from focusing on the speech sounds that are a central element to phonics instruction); an appropriate climate and aesthetics (addressing both of these classroom characteristics would set the occasion for students engaging in school social behaviors that contribute to an overall atmosphere that is conducive to effective instruction); plus, the use of efficient and purposeful routines (routinely employing the elements of explicit instruction not only allow for the efficient use of time but also contribute to the phenomena of students "learning how to learn;" other routines, such as the steps students are to follow to prepare for the start of the lesson and to transition to the next lesson simultaneously teach students appropriate school social behaviors in that context/classroom).

It is important to establish a curriculum that is comprised of the skills in the five domains that pertain to phonemic awareness, phonics, fluency, vocabulary, and reading comprehension. One component of an evidence-based practice that is specific to an academic discipline is teaching students the essential content that comprises the discipline. Research has identified the content students must learn via beginning reading instruction in order to become a proficient reader.

Presenting lessons that incorporate instructional strategies that are based on universal effective teaching practices (e.g., at the outset of the lesson give clear statements of the learning objectives, frequent opportunities for active student response, behavior-specific feedback following student responses) and evidence-based practices specific to the academic discipline (i.e., content pertaining to the five big ideas of reading is taught via explicit instruction).

The teacher effectively manages time to ensure that the content is addressed from "bell to bell," meaning employing every minute of the time allocated for beginning reading instruction along with the use of strategies that addresses each student's need for engaged and academic learning time.

Using formative and summative assessment data (a) to identify each student's level and rate of acquisition of targeted learning outcomes that are directly related to the five big ideas of beginning reading instruction as well as (b) to inform instruction. In terms of informing instruction two uses of the data would be to cause teachers to consider which aspects of their attempt to provide high quality instruction needed to be maintained versus refined and to determine which students need to be provided Tier 2 or Tier 3 services.

CHAPTER 3 COMPREHENSION CHECK

Now that you have finished reading the chapter, you should be able to:

- Discuss the relationship between the terms "scientifically based instruction" and "evidence-based practices."
- Explain what the term "evidence-based practices" refers to.

- Discuss the scientific method and what a researcher is trying to discover in an experiment.
- Explain the relationship between an independent and dependent variable in an experiment.
- List three general types of experimental research designs in education.
- Explain the protocol that is followed to identify an evidence-based practice (EBP).
- Discuss how a general education teacher can combine universal effective interventions and discipline specific instructional strategies to present high-quality, scientifically based beginning reading instruction.

NOTES

1. Bryan G. Cook and Sara Cothren Cook, "Unraveling Evidence-Based Practices in Special Education," *The Journal of Special Education* 47, no. 2 (2013): 71–82.

2. Mitchell L. Yell, *The Law and Special Education*, third edition, ed. Jeffrey Johnston (Upper Saddle River, NJ: Pearson Education, Inc. 2012).

3. Ibid.

4. P. S. Strain and G. Dunlap, "Recommended Practices: Being an Evidence-Based Practitioner," (2006): 2006, http://challengingbehavior.fmhi.usf.edu/handouts/Practitioner.pdf.

5. Melody Tankersley, Sanna Harjusola-Webb, and Timothy J. Landrum, "Using Single-Subject Research to Establish the Evidence Base of Special Education," *Intervention in School and Clinic* 44, no. 2 (2008): 83–90.

6. National Autism Center, "Evidence-Based Practice and Autism in the Schools: A Guide to Providing Appropriate Interventions to Students with Autism Spectrum Disorders," (2009).

7. Bryan Cook, Virginia Buysse, Janette Klingner, Tim Landrum, Robin McWilliam, Melody Tankersley, and Dave Test, "Council for Exceptional Children: Standards for Evidence-Based Practices in Special Education," *Teaching Exceptional Children* 46, no. 6 (2014): 206.

8. Bryan G. Cook, Timothy J. Landrum, Lysandra Cook, and Melody Tankersley, "Introduction to the Special Issue: Evidence-Based Practices in Special Education," *Intervention in School and Clinic* 44, no. 2 (2008): 67.

9. Connie Wong, Samuel L. Odom, Kara Hume, Ann W. Cox, Angel Fettig, Suzanne Kucharczyk, and T. R. Schultz, "Evidence-Based Practices for Children, Youth, and Young Adults with Autism Spectrum Disorder," Chapel Hill: The University of North Carolina, (Frank Porter Graham Child Development Institute, Autism Evidence-Based Practice Review Group, 2014).

10. Bryan G. Cook, Melody Tankersley, and Timothy J. Landrum, "Determining Evidence-Based Practices in Special Education," *Exceptional Children* 75, no. 3 (2009): 365–383.

11. Bryan G. Cook and Sara Cothren Cook, "Unraveling Evidence-Based Practices in Special Education," *The Journal of Special Education* 47, no. 2 (2013): 71–82.

12. Lysandra Cook, Bryan G. Cook, Timothy J. Landrum, and Melody Tankersley, "Examining the Role of Group Experimental Research in Establishing Evidenced-Based Practices," *Intervention in School and Clinic* 44, no. 2 (2008): 76–82.

13. National Autism Center, "Evidence-Based Practice and Autism in the Schools: A Guide to Providing Appropriate Interventions to Students with Autism Spectrum Disorders," (2009).

14. Connie Wong, Samuel L. Odom, Kara Hume, Ann W. Cox, Angel Fettig, Suzanne Kucharczyk, and T. R. Schultz, "Evidence-Based Practices for Children, Youth, and Young Adults with Autism Spectrum Disorder," Chapel Hill: The University of North Carolina, (Frank Porter Graham Child Development Institute, Autism Evidence-Based Practice Review Group, 2014).

15. Bryan G. Cook, Melody Tankersley, Lysandra Cook, and Timothy J. Landrum, "Evidence-Based Practices in Special Education: Some Practical Considerations," *Intervention in School and Clinic,* 44, no. 2 (2008): 69–75.

16. Bryan G. Cook, Melody Tankersley, and Sanna Harjusola-Webb, "Evidence-Based Special Education and Professional Wisdom: Putting It All Together," *Intervention in School and Clinic* 44, no. 2 (2008): 105–111.

17. James McLeskey, Council for Exceptional Children, and Collaboration for Effective Educator Development, Accountability and Reform, *High-Leverage Practices in Special Education.* Arlington, VA: Council for Exceptional Children, 2017.

18. Caroline Torres, Cynthia A. Farley, and Bryan G. Cook, "A Special Educator's Guide to Successfully Implementing Evidence-Based Practices," *Teaching Exceptional Children* 47, no. 2 (2014): 85–93.

19. Debra M. Kamps and Charles R. Greenwood, "Formulating Secondary-Level Reading Interventions," *Journal of Learning Disabilities* 38, no. 6 (November/December 2005): 500–509.

20. Louisa Cook Moats, *Speech to Print: Language Essentials for Teachers,* second edition, (Baltimore, MD: Paul H. Brooks Publishing Company, 2010).

21. Louisa Cook Moats, "Teaching Reading Is Rocket Science: What Expert Teachers of Reading Should Know and Be Able To Do," Washington, DC: American Federation of Teachers, (Item no. 39-0372), (1999).

22. Marilyn J. Adams, "Beginning to Read: Learning and Thinking About Print," Cambridge, MA: MIT Press, 1990.

23. National Reading Panel (US), National Institute of Child Health, and Human Development (US), *Teaching Children to Read: An Evidence-Based Assessment of the Scientific Research Literature on Reading and Its Implications for Reading Instruction,* (National Institute of Child Health and Human Development, National Institutes of Health, 2000). http://www.nationalreadingpanel.org/Publications/summary.htm.

24. National Research Council, *Preventing Reading Difficulties in Young Children,* National Academies Press, 1998, https://doi.org/10.17226/6023.

25. Louisa Cook Moats and Carol Tolman, *The Challenge of Learning to Read,* second edition, Longmont, CO: Sopris West Educational Services, 2009, 57.

26. Debra M. Kamps and Charles R. Greenwood, "Formulating Secondary-Level Reading Interventions," *Journal of Learning Disabilities* 38, no. 6 (November/December 2005): 500–509.

27. Linnea C. Ehri and Alison G. Soffer, "Graphophonemic Awareness: Development in Elementary Students," *Scientific Studies of Reading* 3, no. 1 (1999): 1–30.

28. Barbara R. Foorman, David J. Francis, Jack M. Fletcher, Christopher Schatschneider, and Paras Mehta, "The Role of Instruction in Learning to Read: Preventing Reading Failure in At-Risk Children," *Journal of Educational Psychology* 90, no. 1 (1998): 37.

29. Mary Abbott, Cheryl Walton, and Charles R. Greenwood, "Phonemic Awareness in Kindergarten and First Grade," *Teaching Exceptional Children* 34, no. 4 (2001): 20–26.

30. Brian Byrne and Ruth Fielding-Barnsley, "Evaluation of a Program to Teach Phonemic Awareness to Young Children: A 1-Year Follow-Up," *Journal of Educational Psychology* 85, no. 1 (1993): 104–111.

31. Barbara R. Foorman, David J. Francis, Jack M. Fletcher, Christopher Schatschneider, and Paras Mehta, "The Role of Instruction in Learning to Read: Preventing Reading Failure in At-Risk Children," *Journal of Educational Psychology* 90, no. 1 (1998): 37.

32. Mary Abbott, Cheryl Walton, and Charles R. Greenwood, "Phonemic Awareness in Kindergarten and First Grade," *Teaching Exceptional Children* 34, no. 4 (2001): 20–26.

33. Rebecca H. Felton and Pamela P. Pepper, "Early Identification and Intervention of Phonological Deficits in Kindergarten and Early Elementary Children at Risk for Reading Disability," *School Psychology Review* (1995).

34. Marilyn J. Adams, "Beginning to Read: Learning and Thinking About Print," Cambridge, MA: MIT Press, 1990.

35. Ibid.

36. Mary Abbott, Cheryl Walton, Yolanda Tapia, and Charles R. Greenwood, "Research to Practice: A "Blueprint" for Closing the Gap in Local Schools," *Exceptional Children* 83 (1999): 339–362.

37. Charles R. Greenwood, Barbara Terry, Carmen Arreaga-Mayer, and Rebecca Finney, "The Classwide Peer Tutoring Program: Implementation Factors Moderating Students' Achievement," *Journal of Applied Behavior Analysis* 25, no. 1 (1992): 101–116.

38. Joseph K. Torgesen, Ann W. Alexander, Richard K. Wagner, Carol A. Rashotte, Kytja KS Voeller, and Tim Conway, "Intensive Remedial Instruction for Children with Severe Reading Disabilities: Immediate and Long-Term Outcomes from Two Instructional Approaches," *Journal of Learning Disabilities* 34, no. 1 (2001): 33–58.

39. Siegfried Engelmann, "Theory of Mastery and Acceleration," *Issues in Educating Students with Disabilities* (1997): 117–195.

40. Russell Gersten, Douglas Carnine, and John Woodward, "Direct Instruction Research: The Third Decade," *Remedial and Special Education* 8, no. 6 (1987): 48–56.

41. Rollanda E. O'Connor, Angela Notari-Syverson, and Patricia F. Vadasy, "Ladders to Literacy: The Effects of Teacher-Led Phonological Activities for Kindergarten Children With and Without Disabilities," *Exceptional Children* 63, no. 1 (1996): 117–130.

42. Debra M. Kamps and Charles R. Greenwood, "Formulating Secondary-Level Reading Interventions," *Journal of Learning Disabilities* 38, no. 6 (November/December 2005): 500–509.

43. David J. Chard and Edward J. Kameenui. "Struggling First-Grade Readers: The Frequency and Progress of Their Reading," *The Journal of Special Education* 34, no. 1 (2000): 28–38.

44. Linnea C. Ehri, "Development of the Ability to Read Words," *Handbook of Reading Research* 2, Mohawk, NJ: Lawrence Earlbaum Associates, Publishers (1991): 383–417.

45. Connie Juel, "Learning to Read and Write: A Longitudinal Study of 54 Children from First Through Fourth Grades," *Journal of Educational Psychology* 80, no. 4 (1988): 437.

Chapter Four

Tier 2 Interventions

OVERVIEW

In this chapter you will learn about the primary features of Tier 2 services in an RTI framework: small group instruction and intensive intervention. Key points from the chapter include the following:

Tier 2 services are provided to students who have been identified, through the administration of a screening instrument, as being at-risk for mastering grade-level learning objectives or whose progress monitoring data while being provided Tier 1 services indicate that they are significantly behind their peers in terms of the amount of targeted learning outcomes they have attained which, in turn, indicates that their rate of learning is insufficient.

Students who receive Tier 2 services will continue to receive Tier 1 services. Hence, Tier 2 services are to be designed to supplement Tier 1 services in a way that does not result in "more of the same" instruction that was ineffective in Tier 1.

The two primary features of Tier 2 services are the use of small group arrangements and an increase in the intensity of instruction. Altogether these services focus on the provision of remedial instruction.

Intensive instruction refers to strategically designed interventions that consist of a number of elements that allow for more individualized and prolonged student engagement.

The two approaches to Tier 2 services involve the implementation of either a standard treatment protocol or a problem-solving protocol. A standard treatment protocol consists of the use of a pre-packaged, research-validated program that has been designed to address one or more academic skills or school social behaviors. A problem-solving protocol consists of a school-based team of professionals who work through a multi-step process on behalf of each student who exhibits an academic or school social behavior deficit and develops a corresponding individualized remediation program.

Tier 2 services may differ from Tier 1 services in terms of what are referred to as quantitative changes to interventions. These types of changes can be depicted numerically and tend to be the first type of changes made to differentiate Tier 2 services from Tier 1 services. Quantitative changes include decreasing group size and increasing the (a) frequency and duration of instruction, (b) amount of student responding, (c) use of prompting, (d) frequency of descriptive and specific feedback and (e) frequency of progress monitoring assessment.

Tier 2 services can also involve qualitative changes, which involve descriptions—that are not readily quantifiable—of how Tier 2 services differ from Tier 1 services. These qualitative changes include decreasing the heterogeneity among the students who comprise a small group; arranging the environment so that it allows for teaching and learning that is somewhat unique to a small group arrangement; employing interventions that specifically account for students' characteristics of thinking and learning; writing learning objectives that are more precisely aligned with students' instructional needs; presenting feedback that is more descriptive, specific, and individualized; and, improving the instructor's knowledge and skills.

The dimensions of high-quality instruction can be applied to small group arrangements in ways that increase the probability that Tier 2 services will be more effective and efficient than Tier 1 services by allowing for things such as observational and incidental learning, an emphasis on teaching a more well-defined and focused curriculum, individualized active student responding, and more frequent assessment that informs instruction.

Quantitative and qualitative changes can be refined for students who have been receiving Tier 2 services yet continue to display significant and persistent learning challenges, and do not qualify for the receipt of special education services. In a three-tier model such as the one described in this book these Tier 2 services can be referred to as ultra-intensive.

OVERVIEW OF TIER 2 INTERVENTION SERVICES

To develop an in depth understanding of an RTI framework you must be able to (a) delineate the tiered intervention services that are provided beyond Tier 1 and (b) explain both how and why they are related to, yet different from, Tier 1 services. While the total number of tiers in any two response-to-intervention frameworks may differ, each framework is essentially the same with respect to the general aspects of its first two tiers.

As was explained in chapters 1–3, Tier 1 services in every response-to-intervention framework are presented in the general education classroom and are characterized as high-quality instruction that is predicated on evidence-based practices. In a typical public-school general education classroom, this instruction is presented using a large group arrangement (i.e., a pupil:teacher ratio of 20–30+:1).

Tier 2 services will supplement these Tier 1 services. Among other things, this means that the students who receive Tier 2 services will continue to participate in related Tier 1 activities. Also, a predicate of Tier 2 services is that they are presented to students in small group arrangements and are said to involve increasing the intensity of instruction. This is also known as intensive intervention.

Considering how Tier 1 services have been characterized and their relationship to Tier 2 services, some basic questions about Tier 2 services that you need to be able answer include the following:

1. Which students receive these services, and who provides them (i.e., the students and staff involved)?
2. Why are the services provided (i.e., the purpose of Tier 2 services)?
3. What services are provided? In particular, in what ways are they related to, yet different from, the Tier 1 services that have not proven to be effective (i.e., the characteristics of Tier 2 services)?
4. When, during the school day, are Tier 2 services provided?
5. Where are these services provided (i.e., the location)?

Students and Staff Involved

One way that Tier 2 services differ from Tier 1 services is in terms of who is involved. With respect to the students who receive these services, in an RTI framework Tier 2 intervention services are provided to students (a) who have been identified as being significantly at risk for failure based on their performance on a screening assessment or (b) whose progress monitoring data while being provided Tier 1 services indicate that they are significantly behind their peers in terms of the amount of expected learning outcomes attained and the rate at which new material is learned. Reportedly 20–25 percent of the students in a typical classroom will need to receive Tier 2 services.

The staff who might provide Tier 2 services can vary greatly from school to school. It is directly related to a primary feature of some Tier 2 services, which is that they are provided to students in a small group arrangement with the use of a standard-treatment protocol that provides the instructor with detailed guidelines regarding how to present a lesson. A standard treatment protocol is explained below in the section titled "Intervention Services Provided."

The range of personnel who might provide Tier 2 services include school employees and others who are not employed by the school. School employees may include the student's general education classroom teacher; an intervention specialist, meaning a teacher who has specialized training in the presentation of academic or social behavior interventions (i.e., a reading therapist, math coach, or behavior specialist); a general interventionist, meaning a teacher who has been hired to implement either Tier 2 academic interventions, social behavior interventions, or both; and a teacher assistant. Non-paid personnel may include retired adult volunteers, preservice teachers, or even a high school student who is earning community service hours.

Purpose of Tier 2 Services

Tier 2 involves the provision of remedial services that target the expected learning outcomes that a student has not attained. This means that during the time that a student is provided Tier 2 services he will work to attain the same academic and school social behavior standards that are the focus of Tier 1 services. This focus of Tier 2 intervention services highlights what has been called the logic of RTI, which calls for all levels of the framework beyond Tier 1 to provide the intensive intervention that is necessary to enable a student to return to the general education classroom where he will achieve satisfactorily at grade level while only receiving Tier 1 services. [1,2]

Intervention Services Provided

Standard Treatment or Problem-Solving Protocol

In general, Tier 2 services are provided in accordance with one of two approaches: either a standard treatment protocol or a problem-solving protocol. A standard treatment protocol involves the use of a pre-packaged, research-validated intervention that has been designed to address a specific academic or school social behavior deficit (e.g., phonics skills, asking appropriate questions in class). This means that the instructor presents this intervention to every student in the small group "as it has been designed."

Some have referred to these protocols as scripted programs given the fact that a number of them not only provide the teacher with the instructional materials that they are to use but also the dialogue they are to present to the students and the pace of instruction that is to be followed. Among other things the use of a standard treatment protocol means the small group must be homogeneous with respect to each student's learning deficit.

A problem-solving protocol consists of a school-based team of professionals who work through a multi-step process on behalf of each student who exhibits an academic deficit or is not engaging in appropriate school social behavior. This process begins with the identification of the student's academic achievement or school social behavior deficit followed by an examination of various aspects of the deficit (e.g., what is the extent of the deficit, which interventions have already been used to address it, etc.).

An individualized intervention plan is then designed and implemented, and student performance data are routinely collected and evaluated to determine the plan's effectiveness. Unlike the standard treatment protocol, a problem-solving protocol allows for the use of a variety of interventions that are based on a student's unique deficits and performance data.

Small Group, Intensive Intervention

Regardless which of the two approaches are used, according to the RTI framework, Tier 2 services are to be provided in a small group arrangement and in a way that involves increasing the intensity of instruction relative to the instruction that is presented in Tier 1. Interestingly, the use of a small group arrangement is one way to increase the intensity of instruction. Since the term small group instruction is used quite often to refer the delivery of instruction using these arrangements, throughout this book this term is used interchangeably with the term small group arrangement.

Intensive instruction refers to strategically designed interventions that consist of a number of elements that allow for more individualized and prolonged student engagement. Prolonged student engagement results from actions that keep the student cognitively processing the content that is the focus of instruction.

Examples of these actions include (a) repeatedly directing the student to attend to activities that are at, or only slightly above, his instructional level; (b) having him respond more often than he typically does in large group arrangements—both directly via a mode of active student responding or indirectly through active participation in observational and incidental learning; and, (c) providing him with feedback that is specific to both his correct and incorrect responses. The goal is for this individualized and prolonged student engagement to result in both a higher level and rate of student attainment of the targeted learning outcomes than was the case when less intensive, large group instruction was presented in Tier 1.

The elements of intensive instruction have been described in terms of the types of changes that can differentiate Tier 1 and Tier 2 services such that the Tier 2 services are effective for their purpose. The two types of changes have been classified as either quantitative or qualitative changes. A number of these quantitative and qualitative changes are listed and described below.

It is important to remain mindful of the fact that in an RTI framework the characteristics of the various tiers distinguish them from each other yet also allow for the tiers to be logically connected. As you read the information below about some of the characteristics of Tier 2 services that differentiate them from Tier 1, remain mindful of the fact that students who will be provided supplemental Tier 2 services will continue to receive Tier 1 services that will, in some way, address their academic or social behavior deficit, and that the logic of RTI is to have students who receive Tier 2 services return to Tier 1 where they subsequently will attain targeted learning outcomes solely as the result of receiving Tier 1 services.

Quantitative changes

Quantitative changes involve a readily identifiable numerical aspect of an intervention and are the most immediate changes employed in Tier 2. Examples of these changes include, but certainly are not limited to (a) decreasing group size, (b) increasing the frequency and duration of the intervention, and (c) increasing active student responding, (d) the use of prompts, (e) the provision of descriptive feedback about students' responses, and (f) the frequency of progress monitoring. Information about each of these quantitative changes is presented below.

1. Decreasing group size. The first element of intensive instruction that sets the stage for more individualized and prolonged student engagement is the use of a small group arrangement. For the purposes of this book, this arrangement is defined as a pupil to teacher ratio that involves two to eight students per instructor.

   A small group arrangement allows for the unique implementation of a number of the elements described here and that have been shown to permit students to attain targeted learning outcomes that were not realized under the conditions in a general education classroom. These elements can be manipulated for the purpose of changing the intensity of instruction. This topic is discussed later in this chapter.

2. Increasing the frequency and duration of instruction. When students are classified as needing Tier 2 services they are allocated more time to receive instruction that pertains to the area in which they have not attained targeted learning outcomes—such as reading, math, and writing—or the school social behavior. This means that both the frequency and duration of this instruction will increase.

   For instance, in a situation where math instruction had been presented to a student during one seventy-five-minute block per day, when the student begins receiving Tier 2 services he will participate in this block plus the block of time that has been established for Tier 2 services on the days of the week when these services will be provided. Likewise, the total amount of time, or duration, that the student will participate in math instruction will increase because the time spent receiving Tier 2 services will be in addition to the time spent receiving Tier 1 services.

The number of days per week that a student will be provided Tier 2 services as well as the length of time these services will be provided each day will vary across schools' response-to-intervention frameworks. A basic arrangement is for a student to be provided Tier 2 services two to three days per week for thirty to forty-five minutes per day.

For example, these services would be provided during a regularly scheduled block of time at the end of the school day during which every student participates in an activity referred to as "What I Need." During this block students across the entire school would receive some type of individualized instruction such as enrichment activities, assistance completing unfinished classroom work, and Tier 2 services as remedial, small-group instruction for the students who need to receive them.

3. Increasing active student responding. Active student responding refers to students' displays of overt behaviors to indicate their responses to a teacher's questions that are posed for the purpose of gauging how well students are comprehending the lesson.

4. Additionally, requiring active student responding is one strategy for keeping students engaged in a lesson by getting them to cognitively process the instructional content.

There are many forms of active student responding, and a number of them can be used similarly in large and small group arrangements. For instance, a teacher can pose a True or False question and direct all of the students to respond at the same time by showing a thumbs up if they believe the correct answer is true or a thumbs down if they believe the answer is false.

This type of simultaneous responding is called unison, or choral, responding. In most instances when a general education teacher requires this type of response she intends to get a general idea regarding whether the class, as a whole, is comprehending her instruction rather than closely assessing the responses of individual students.

In the small group arrangements that are used in Tier 2 the teacher can present more opportunities for active student responding as well as closely assess the responses of individual students. The teacher can do both because, due to its size, she will spend less time scanning the group and will have to keep track of fewer responses. This is particularly the case when the pupil:teacher ratio is 2–4:1 as opposed to 5–8:1. Also, when the pupil:teacher ratio is 2–4:1 the teacher can require individual rather than choral responding.

This aspect of small group instruction applies to the next three changes that are discussed below. That is, reducing the number of students in an instructional grouping will set the occasion for the teacher to increase her use of a number of effective strategies, including active student responding, prompting, and the presentation of descriptive feedback.

5. Increasing prompting for desirable behavior. A prompt is defined as additional information that a teacher presents, after delivering the task directive, to increase the probability that a student will provide a correct response/respond correctly.

   For example, when a teacher is instructing students about reading consonant-vowel-consonant words, she might show a student an index card on which the word "cat" is written and simultaneously present the task directive, "Read this word." To increase the probability that the student will read the word correctly, she says the first two sounds of the word that are represented by the letters c and a.

   This information that is presented after the task directive is a prompt. The small group arrangement that is used in Tier 2 will enable the teacher to provide more prompts as well as individualize the prompts to meet each student's needs.

6. Increasing the frequency of descriptive, specific feedback. The information that a teacher presents to students after they provide a response is referred to as feedback. Among other things it lets the student know whether his response was correct. Feedback can be described in terms of a number of features, including whether it is feedback about a correct or incorrect response and is general ("good reading") or descriptive and specific ("correct, you read the word cat").

   The small group arrangement that is used in Tier 2 will enable the teacher to provide more descriptive, specific feedback. By its very nature, this feedback is individualized.

7. Increasing the frequency of progress monitoring. Progress monitoring occurs more frequently in Tier 2 so that the resulting data can readily inform instruction. Since students receiving Tier 2 services are demonstrating noteworthy achievement deficits they cannot be permitted to spend relatively long periods of time engaging in additional ineffective interventions. Hence, progress monitoring known as formative assessment occurs once or twice a week—or several times per month—rather than after a prolonged period of instruction. For instance, in some cases Tier 1 periodic screenings occur only three times per year.

Qualitative changes

Qualitative changes pertain to descriptions about the characteristics of Tier 2 services more than counts or measures of the characteristics of these services. Yet, changes to the characteristics of Tier 2 services that are considered to be qualitative compliment quantitative changes and contribute to the quantitative learning outcomes attained.

Examples of qualitative changes are listed and explained below. These include:[3]

1. Decreasing the heterogeneity among the students who comprise a small group
2. Arranging the environment so that it allows for teaching and learning that is somewhat unique to small group arrangements
3. Employing interventions that specifically account for the students' characteristics of thinking and learning
4. Defining learning objectives that are more precisely aligned with students' instructional needs
5. Presenting individualized, descriptive, specific feedback
6. Improving the instructor's knowledge and skills

As you read the explanations for each description it is important that you remember that the point of reference for each qualitative change is Tier 1 and the manner in which services are being provided in large group arrangements in a general education classroom. Some of these services are described to enhance your understanding of the types of qualitative changes that can be made in Tier 2.[4]

1. Decreasing the heterogeneity among the students who comprise a small group. A homogeneous group refers to one in which the students are similar in a number of key respects while a heterogeneous group is one in which the students are dissimilar. Homogeneity and heterogeneity can, therefore, be thought of as opposite sides of the same coin.

    a. In most public schools, students are randomly assigned to general education classrooms, which often results in significant diversity among the students in terms of their levels of performance and rates of learning. In an RTI framework one way to differentiate Tier 2 from Tier 1 services is to reduce the diversity among the students who are grouped together for instruction.
    b. In Tier 2 teachers are expected to take great care in selecting which students will receive instruction at the same time in a

small group. The reason for doing so is because small group
instruction will be more efficient and effective when the
students in the group have more in common with respect to
the content they need to learn and how they go about processing information and indicating their understanding of it.

2. Arranging the environment so that it allows for teaching and learning
that is somewhat unique to small group arrangements. The physical
arrangement for small group instruction can set the occasion for the
use of instructional strategies that are more easily employed in this
arrangement because of the relative close proximity of the teacher and
students as compared to their proximity in a general education classroom.

   For instance, if the environment is arranged so that every student in
the group can readily observe all of the other students in the group,
this arrangement will increase the probability that observational learning will occur—provided the teacher is aware of this possibility and
systematically plans for it. Observational learning occurs when a student attains a targeted learning outcome that has been established for
another student in the group after the first student observes the second
student correctly perform the skill and receive reinforcement for doing
so.

3. Employing interventions that specifically account for the students'
characteristics of thinking and learning. Being able to determine
which students will be in a group enables teachers to decide upon, and
use, interventions that can address the characteristics of thinking and
learning that are exhibited by the students more so than is the case in a
general education classroom. For instance, if the students in the group
are prone to distractions, challenged to process oral language, and
respond optimally to an exceedingly structured environment, the
teacher could account for these characteristics of thinking and learning
as described below.

   a. Prone to distractions. If small group instruction is conducted
   within the general education classroom the teacher could
   seat students so that their backs are facing their classmates
   and position portable dividers to block anything that might
   be seen in front of, or to the sides of, the students.

   b. Processing oral language. The teacher could provide single-
   step, rather than multi-step directives as well as intentional
   pauses to give students extra time to process her oral language.

c. Structure. Structure refers to a teacher systematically directing all instructional activities, to include deciding the tasks students will perform, how they will perform them, and for how long. Elements of structure could include routines for entering and exiting the group and the use of a lesson plan that is based upon the tenets of explicit instruction (see chapter 2).

4. Defining learning objectives that are more precisely aligned with students' instructional needs. Tier 2 services are designed to address the specific skills a student has not mastered and provide the student with the repetition—both in terms receiving the same [or very similar] instruction repeatedly and practicing targeted skills—that he needs to attain his targeted learning outcomes.

   This means the Tier 2 curriculum is to be much narrower in scope than is the Tier 1 curriculum. In Tier 1, students work to attain rather broadly stated learning outcomes from a curriculum whose scope and sequence, along with its pacing guide, result in the presentation of instruction at a rate that is not well aligned with some students' characteristics of thinking and learning.

5. Presenting individualized, descriptive, specific feedback. During small group instruction the teacher is in a more tenable position to provide individualized, descriptive, specific feedback following student responses to questions that a teacher poses to assess the students' understanding of a lesson than is the case in a large group arrangement. This is so whether the students who comprise a small group respond in unison or individually.

   Given the pupil to teacher ratio in a general education classroom, a teacher will be challenged to provide feedback that is specific to each student's response. More often than not the teacher will provide general feedback or feedback that is specific to one student's response, such as the student who was called upon to solve a math problem on the board at the front of the class.

6. Improving the instructor's knowledge and skills. As Tier 2 services are being designed and subsequently implemented there are a number of variables specific to the instructor that can be addressed in an attempt to improve the quality of the instruction (i.e., its efficiency and effectiveness) that is presented—both in its own right and relative to Tier 1 instruction. These variables include an instructor's knowledge and teaching skills with respect to (a) the academic content being taught, (b) use of interventions that are particularly suited for small group instruction (e.g., prompting, active student responding, individ-

ualized feedback, observational and incidental learning), behavior management, and diagnostic assessment.

Time of the Day When Tier 2 Services are Provided

When a student has been determined to need Tier 2 services more time during the school day is allocated to the presentation of instruction that addresses the student's academic achievement or school social behavior deficit. This occurs as a result of the student continuing to receive Tier 1 services while also receiving additional Tier 2 services. Not surprisingly, there are numerous ways to schedule these additional services.

As was explained previously, a basic arrangement is to designate a block of time (thirty to forty-five minutes) at the end of the school day during which every student participates in an activity referred to as, "What I Need." During this time some students in the school would participate in enrichment activities, some would complete unfinished general education classroom work, and Tier 2 students would receive remedial, small-group instruction.

Location of Tier 2 Service Provision

Just as there are many ways to schedule the provision of Tier 2 services there are also many locations where these services can be provided. In some instances, the general education teacher provides Tier 2 services in her classroom.

However, given the need for a general education teacher to focus on the provision of high-quality, Tier 1 instruction while also addressing numerous administrative tasks, it is questionable whether this teacher can also effectively present the Tier 2 services that are called for in a response-to-intervention framework. Thus, for the purposes of this book, Tier 2 services are explained in terms of an instructor other than the student's general education teacher providing these services—either in the classroom or elsewhere in the school. These instructors were identified previously.

Outside of the general education classroom, Tier 2 services may be provided elsewhere in the school or on the school's campus. These locations include a classroom that has been configured for small group instruction; a dual use location, such as the cafeteria; or, a detached building, such as a portable trailer.

SMALL GROUP INSTRUCTION: A PRIMER

A theme that runs throughout a response-to-intervention framework is that the services that are provided in each successive tier will differ in ways that are calculated to increase the probability that they will be effective with the students who are receiving them. An easily defined and identifiable way that Tier 2 services will differ from Tier 1 services is the size of the instructional group.

Simply stated, small group instruction is a hallmark characteristic of not only Tier 2 services but also many Tier 3 services. Thus, to develop a fundamental understanding of an RTI framework it is important for you to be cognizant of issues that pertain to the design and implementation of small group instruction.

The extent to which Tier 2 services will differ from Tier 1 services and have a higher probability of being effective with the students who receive them will depend, to a large degree, on how adroit an instructor is at making use of the quantitative and qualitative changes that can be made to Tier 1 services so that the effective, intensive intervention that a small group arrangement allows for can be realized. Hence, the purpose of this section is to make you aware of some basic topics you can address for the purpose of making Tier 2 small group instruction more intense, effective, and differential in comparison to Tier 1 services. The topics come from those that were addressed in chapter 2's discussion of an operational definition for Tier 1 high-quality instruction.

Environmental Arrangement

For the most part the same environmental arrangement principles that were discussed in chapter 2 will apply to the arrangement of the environment in which small group instruction will be presented. However, these principles need to be applied with a consideration of the ways that small group instruction will differ from the large group instruction that is presented in the general education classroom.

Additionally, the location where Tier 2 small group instruction will be presented will dictate some unique environmental arrangement matters that must be addressed. This will be the case when this instruction is either presented in a general education classroom or else in another location within a school (e.g., the cafeteria) where potentially distracting stimuli that are extraneous to the specific area within which small group instruction is being presented are pervasive. This matter is addressed in the discussion below:

1. *Lines of sight.* A small group arrangement provides an opportunity for the teacher to be in close proximity to each of her students. Likewise, each of the students can be in close proximity to one another. Consequently, the teacher needs to arrange the environment in a way that will enhance the effectiveness of the instruction that is presented because this proximity provides opportunities for doing so.

From the teacher's perspective a small group arrangement allows her to more closely observe each student she instructs. Among other things this circumstance will enable the teacher to (a) monitor and respond to each student's displays of social behavior that both contributes to the group's cohesion and complies with class rules and (b) gauge how well each student is processing the content that is to be learned.

From the student's perspective the small group arrangement not only enables him to easily see the teacher and any instructional materials that are the focus of the lesson but also see every other student such that there is an enhanced probability that observational and incidental learning will occur. Observational learning was defined previously. Incidental learning refers to learning that occurs when a student acquires information that is presented during a lesson but is not directly tied to any instructional strategy, meaning it is not a part of instructional strategies that involve things such as the presentation of reinforcement or teacher feedback.

To realize the potential benefits of clear lines of sight to both the teacher and the students, the students should sit in a semi-circle facing the teacher, who will be seated or will stand near the midpoint. Horseshoe and kidney-shaped tables are configured for this purpose. Likewise, students can be seated around a circular table such that their positions form a semi-circle with the teacher in the middle. Chairs and desks also can be positioned in this manner, or several rectangular tables can be connected to form a u-shape with the teacher positioned in the middle.

While creating clear lines of sight and accounting for the close proximity that small group arrangements allow can enable you to benefit from these potentially advantageous aspects of small group arrangements, there are a number of potential downsides to the close proximity that is afforded by small group arrangements. One is that students might more easily come into physical contact with each other, leading to an escalation of the situation when a student who has been inadvertently touched responds in kind. Another is that the close proximity might result in an increase in the number of potentially distracting stimuli in the area where the group is being instructed, while a third is that the close proximity makes it easier to dishonestly claim credit for a classmate's answer.

2. *Having instructional materials nearby and ready to use.* Having instructional materials nearby allows a teacher to stay engaged with students in multiple ways that would not be possible if she were to have to leave the group repeatedly to get these materials from another location within the classroom. Having instructional materials nearby

and ready to use is critically important to the effective and efficient operation of small group instruction since, depending on the characteristics of the students who comprise the group and whether a standard treatment or problem solving protocol is being followed, managing these materials can present the teacher with a significant challenge relative to performing this task in a large group arrangement in a general education classroom.

If the group is homogeneous in terms of the content the students are learning, and a standard treatment protocol is used, then the teacher can plan for managing the use of the materials in much the same way as would be done in a general education classroom. Yet, if the group is heterogeneous, particularly with respect to the content they are learning to master, and a problem-solving protocol is used, then managing instructional materials can present a newfound challenge.

For example, if the students are working to master two beginning literacy skills—reading high frequency words and the sound-symbol relationship (i.e., phonics) for short vowel sounds encoded with a single letter—but each student needs to learn a slightly different set of words as well as slightly different phonics skills—then the teacher may have to plan for the use of similar yet different materials during one part of the lesson and then transition to another set of materials (which are likewise similar yet different) during another part of the lesson.

3. *Classroom aesthetics.* As is the case for a general education classroom, the overall aesthetics of the location where small group instruction will be presented needs to be addressed since the aesthetics might possibly function as an antecedent to the students' engagement in appropriate behaviors. This issue may take on even more importance in the case of a student who is displeased with having to participate in Tier 2 services. This student's perceived unpleasant situation could be made even worse if he was required to go to a location that he considered to be drab and uninviting.

4. *Routines.* Teachers should establish routines that will enable them to address issues relevant to Tier 2 small group instruction. Two examples include routines that allow for the use of allocated time and routines that enable students to monitor their own learning.

First, teachers should create routines that will enable them to maximize the time that has been allocated for small group instruction. These routines would include, but not necessarily be limited to, (a) moving efficiently from one location in a general education classroom to the location in that room where small group instruction will be presented, (b) moving efficiently from the general education classroom to a location outside of the classroom where small group instruction will be presented, and (c) how to begin and end a lesson.

Second, a teacher should follow a prescribed routine when she presents instruction so that students can assimilate a process for learning. This phenomenon has been referred to as "learning how to learn." An example of how this could occur would be when a student begins to self-advocate for the type of assistance he needs during the lead component when a model-lead-test lesson presentation protocol is used.

5. *Limit potential distractions.* When small group instruction is presented in a classroom that has been designed, exclusively, for this type of arrangement, the instructor will need to account for potential distracting stimuli similar to the way a general education teacher does. However, when this instruction is presented within a general education classroom or a setting outside of this classroom that is prone to many potentially distracting stimuli, the teacher most likely will need to take several steps to configure the location so as to mediate the impact of these stimuli.

To address visual stimuli, the teacher should seat students so that their backs are facing their classmates in the general education classroom who are not in the small group and position portable dividers to block anything that might be seen in front of, or to the sides of, the students who are in the small group. To address auditory stimuli the teacher should position the small group as far away as possible from sources of sound (e.g., high traffic areas, keyboards, printers, other instructional activities) and coordinate with others (e.g., the teacher of the general education classroom) a method that can be used to modulate individual voice volumes and the overall noise level within the location.

Time Management

When planning for, and subsequently presenting, Tier 2 small group instruction the teacher must continue to account for allocated, engaged, and academic learning time. By emphasizing certain instructional strategies such as directives for attending to the teacher, calling upon students randomly for their responses to a teacher's questions, and prompting students in ways that increase the probability that they will engage in both observational and incidental learning, the teacher can directly address students' engaged time. The amount of each student's academic learning time will depend on how directly all of the learning objectives that are taught to the small group align with a student's learning needs.

Curriculum

Tier 2 services will focus on teaching the content from the core curriculum that a student has not mastered as a result of receiving Tier 1 services which, in accordance with the framework, involve the presentation of high-quality instruction in a general education classroom. Yet, for Tier 2 to be notably different from Tier 1 the Tier 2 curriculum focus will need to be more precisely defined for each student. Zeroing in on the curriculum in this manner will prevent teachers from using valuable instructional time addressing curriculum content that a student has mastered already.

It will be easier for the teacher to present instruction that addresses the specific curriculum content that each student must learn when she works with a relatively homogeneous group. The more that the students in a small group are alike in terms of the academic skills and school social behaviors that they need to attain the more opportunities the teacher will have to address specific curriculum content the students must learn, and the higher the probability that effective instruction will result.[5,6]

Evidence-Base Practices

The instructional strategies that are used in both Tier 1 and Tier 2 are to be evidence-based practices—both universal and subject matter effective practices. What differentiates the two tiers is the manner in which some of the universal, effective, evidence-based practices can be used in Tier 2 because of the reduced pupil to teacher ratio and resulting environmental arrangement that was described previously. Mostly the use of subject specific, effective, evidence-based teaching practices will remain constant across both tiers.

In chapter 2, a number of universal effective teaching practices were identified and explained. Below some of these practices are discussed with respect to how they can be used in a small group arrangement so that they work in concert with other aspects of the interventions in this arrangement (i.e., the unique environmental arrangement plus quantitative and qualitative changes) that are calculated to differentiate Tier 2 from Tier 1 instruction and, at least partly because of this differentiation, enable Tier 2 services to be more effective.

1. *Directive to attend to the teacher.* This directive sets the occasion for observational and incidental learning. The directive also can be given for the purpose of refocusing students on the need to engage in appropriate social behaviors that are specific to Tier 2 small group instruction. The follow-on attention response can serve as the starting point for the further display of group-specific appropriate social behavior.

This behavior is necessary for learning whatever content is the focus of Tier 2 small group instruction: academic or school social behavior.

2. *Prompting.* The use of prompts can be more efficient if all of the students in the group are working to master the same academic skills or school social behavior because only one type of prompt may need to be provided to the students. Conversely, given the pupil to teacher ratio it will be easier to provide individualized prompts.

3. *Active student responding.* The small group arrangement that is used in Tier 2 and a concentrated focus on select, specific curriculum content will enable the teacher to present more opportunities for active student responding as well as closely assess the responses of individual students.

4. *Individualized, descriptive, specific feedback.* The small group arrangement that is used in Tier 2 will enable the teacher to provide more individualized, descriptive, specific feedback. In turn, providing this feedback will set the stage for observational and incidental learning.

Assessment

Care must be taken to conduct assessments that will produce data to inform instruction.[7] The students who are receiving Tier 2 services have already demonstrated that they are challenged to attain grade-level targeted learning outcomes, so there is a pressing need for assessment data to either confirm student progress or contribute to decisions regarding how Tier 2 instruction can be refined so that it is effective. Diagnostic assessments that are aligned to Tier 2 curriculum content may be conducted for these purposes. This type of assessment is covered in chapter 6, which addresses numerous topics that concern assessments within the framework.

Note that some progress monitoring assessment data will be gathered from the activities that students complete in the general education classroom while they simultaneously receive Tier 2 services. However, most of these data will not be as closely aligned to the specific curriculum content that is the focus of these students' Tier 2 services.

Continuum of Knowledge About Presenting Small Group Instruction

The degree to which a teacher needs to be knowledgeable about the intricacies of small group instruction can be thought of as existing along a continuum. One end of the continuum would represent the small group arrangements in which a standard treatment protocol is employed. To the extent that this protocol involves a pre-packaged, highly scripted intervention, the instructor will be more inclined to present instruction as she is directed rather than engage in improvisation by manipulating variables that she has reason to believe will make the instruction more effective.

This depiction of a standard treatment protocol is supported by two facts. One is that a wide variety of adults—to include individuals who have not received any formal training to be a teacher—can be adequately trained to present a standard treatment protocol. The second is that this protocol is to be used with small groups of homogeneous students, meaning each student in the group needs to learn the content that is taught by the protocol (e.g., decoding skills or basic addition facts).

The other end of the continuum would represent the small group arrangements in which some type of problem-solving protocol is employed. Even though problem solving protocols involve the development and implementation of intervention services that are predicated on a case study approach, this practice does not always mean that the services will look markedly different from those that result from the use of a standard treatment protocol.

In a large school a problem-solving protocol may result in intervention services to a homogeneous group of students such as the one described above. Conversely, in a small, rural school a problem-solving protocol may result in services to a very heterogeneous group of students since the options of creating homogeneous groups are limited to non-existent. In this situation the teacher would need to be well-versed in both the art presenting effective small group instruction.

PROVIDING ULTRA INTENSIVE TIER 2 SERVICES

In the three-tier response-to-intervention framework that is explained in this book Tier 3 involves the provision of special education services. Thus, at some point in time a decision will have to be made about whether a student who has received both Tier 1 and Tier 2 services—but continues to demonstrate persistent achievement deficits—needs to be evaluated for the purpose of determining whether he is eligible to receive special education services. While this decision is made on a case-by-case basis a common practice that is followed in many response-to-intervention frameworks is as follows.

Each student who has been identified as needing Tier 2 services must be provided them for a minimum length of time (e.g., nine weeks) unless the student's progress monitoring data indicate that he has attained his targeted learning outcomes before the end of this time and is being successful in the general education classroom while being provided Tier 1 services only. If this is not the case, one of three decisions has to be made:

1. Continue providing the Tier 2 services that are in place for another, similar length of time. This decision would be made on behalf of a student whose Tier 2 assessment data indicate that the student is making progress that, if it continues at its current rate, is projected to result in the student attaining his targeted learning outcomes at the end of the extended time in Tier 2 and then return to the general education classroom while being provided Tier 1 services only.
2. Keep providing the student Tier 2 services but make substantive quantitative and qualitative changes to them because the student's progress monitoring data indicate that both his level and rate of learning are increasing, but only to what could be considered to be a minimal to moderate degree.
3. Refer the student for an evaluation for the purpose of determining whether he meets the eligibility criteria for special education services. This decision would be made on behalf of a student whose Tier 2 assessment data indicate that there is little to no change in the student's level or rate of learning and school personnel do not believe that changes to Tier 2 services will make an appreciable difference to the student's level and rate of learning.

To appropriately address the middle scenario the elements that comprise the Tier 2 intensive intervention will have to be changed in ways that afford the student even more of an opportunity to receive strategically designed interventions that consist of a number of elements that allow for more individualized and prolonged student engagement. Some ways of making these changes are as follows.

1. *Size of the instructional group.* The size of the group can be made as small as possible such that it still meets the definition for group instruction. This would mean that the pupil:teacher ratio is no more than 2–3:1. Resources permitting, a 1:1 arrangement could be used, and some of the small group instructional strategies—such as providing the student with an attention directive, prompts, and specific feedback—could be employed. However, others, such as those that address observational learning, could not.
2. *Frequency of progress monitoring.* Progress monitoring may be conducted daily through the use of probes. Probes are very short assessments that consist of items that solicit students and take one to two minutes to administer. Even if daily probes are not conducted some type of appropriate progress monitoring assessment could be conducted more often than was the case previously, but for the same reasons.

For instance, progress monitoring could be conducted twice per week rather than twice per month. Overall teachers need to balance the need to gather assessment information that both documents student progress and informs instruction against performing assessment activities that take away from a student's academic learning time.

3. *Duration of the intervention.* The duration of each instructional session could be extended. Instead of a thirty to forty-five-minute session, each session could be increased to sixty to seventy-five minutes of instruction.

4. *Frequency with which the intervention is delivered.* Likewise, the number of days per week that Tier 2 services are provided could be extended to four to five days instead of two to three days. These services would continue to be provided in addition to the related Tier 1 services that are being presented in the student's general education classroom.

5. *Focus on the content or skills.* The instruction will continue to address the specific academic skills or school social behaviors a student has not mastered. The learning objectives will become as precise as possible through the use of diagnostic assessments and will be established to increase the probability that the student will demonstrate not only skill mastery but also maintenance.

   Moreover, at this point in time the instructional focus most likely will be on what are considered to be basic, foundational skills. Accordingly, these Tier 2 services would be characterized as remedial instruction whereas the instruction that the student will continue to receive in the general education classroom would provide him with exposure to the grade-level core curriculum that would, in some way, address his targeted learning outcomes and consist of some type of scaffolded instruction.

6. *Teacher or specialist training.* It is as important as ever that the instructor who presents these services should have specialized training and a wealth of experience pertaining to both teaching the content that is the focus of the student's instruction and directing small group arrangements. If this type of instructor had not been providing Tier 2 services previously this is one way that a qualitative change could be made to this more intense intervention.

TIER 2 SERVICES AS SPECIAL EDUCATION

It is possible that some Tier 2 services will be configured in a way that permits them to be special education services for students with disabilities. This circumstance is discussed in the next chapter and highlights a point that was made previously, which is that it can be difficult to distinguish between the needs of a student who exhibits a learning challenge and those of a student who has a specific learning disability.

Regardless whether a student is identified as having a disability, the fact is that some students who demonstrate persistent academic delays have intensive intervention needs that can result in them requiring ten to thirty times as much practice as their typical peers to learn new information.[8] Prior to the creation of the response-to-intervention framework these students who did not qualify for the receipt of special education services and could not access Tier 2 services simply because they were not available were described as "falling through an instructional crack." One outcome of using the framework is the elimination of any such crack.

CHAPTER 4 COMPREHENSION CHECK

Now that you have finished reading the chapter, you should be able to:

- Explain how Tier 2 services are to supplement Tier 1 services.
- Identify the two primary features of Tier 2 services in an RTI framework.
- Discuss the purpose of Tier 2 services.
- Describe the following two approaches to the provision of Tier 2 services: standard treatment and problem-solving protocol.
- Explain what is meant by "intensive instruction."
- Compare and contrast Tier 1 and Tier 2 services with respect to both quantitative and qualitative changes to Tier 1 services.
- Explain how small group instruction is defined in this book.
- Discuss how the five components of high-quality instruction can be applied to small group instruction.
- Discuss how the elements that comprise intensive intervention can be changed to allow for more individualized and prolonged engagement by students who are determined to need Tier 2 services for a relatively long duration.

NOTES

1. Wayne Sailor, "Access to the General Curriculum: Systems Change or Tinker Some More?" *Research and Practice for Persons with Severe Disabilities* 34, no. 1 (2008): 249–257.

2. Wayne Sailor, "Advances in Schoolwide Inclusive School Reform," *Remedial and Special Education* 36, no. 2 (2015): 94–99.

3. National Center on Intensive Intervention (NCII) at American Institutes for Research, *Data-Based Individualization: A Framework for Intensive Intervention*, ERIC Clearinghouse, 2013.

4. Daryl F. Mellard and Evelyn Johnson, *RTI: A Practitioner's Guide to Implementing Response-to-intervention*, (Thousand Oaks, CA: Corwin Press. 2008).

5. Belva C. Collins, David L. Gast, Melinda J. Ault, and Mark Wolery, "Small Group Instruction: Guidelines for Teachers and Students with Moderate to Severe Handicaps," *Education & Training in Mental Retardation* 26, no. 1 (1991): 1–18.

6. Debra M. Kamps, Dale Walker, Erin P. Dugan, Betsy R. Leonard, Susan F. Thibadeau, Kathleen Marshall, Laurie Grossnickle, and Brenda Boland. "Small Group Instruction for School-Aged Students with Autism and Developmental Disabilities," *Focus on Autistic Behavior* 6, no. 4 (1991): 1–18.

7. Russell Gersten, Sybilla Beckmann, Benjamin Clarke, Anne Foegen, Laurel Marsh, Jon R. Star, and Bradley Witzel, "Assisting Students Struggling with Mathematics: Response-to-intervention (RTI) for Elementary and Middle Schools. NCEE 2009-4060," *What Works Clearinghouse* (2009), http://ies.ed.gov/ncee/wwc/publications/practiceguides/.

8. Russell Gersten, Donald Compton, Carol M. Connor, Joseph Dimino, Lana Santoro, Sylvia Linan-Thompson, and W. David Tilly, "Assisting Students Struggling with Reading: Response-to-intervention and Multi-Tier Intervention for Reading in the Primary Grades. A Practice Guide. (NCEE 2009-4045). Washington, DC: National Center for Education Evaluation and Regional Assistance, Institute of Education Sciences, US Department of Education," *National Center for Education Evaluation and Regional Assistance, Institute of Education Services.* (2008), http://ies.ed.gov/ncee/wwc/publications/practiceguides.

Chapter Five

Tier 3—Special Education

OVERVIEW

In this chapter you will learn about special education services and their relationship to the components of an RTI framework. Key points from the chapter include the following:

In the three-tier RTI framework that is described in this book, Tier 3 consists of the provision of special education services.

Special education services were created to provide students with disabilities access to public schools and an opportunity to learn the core curriculum.

In a number of instances, the goal of special education does not involve the elimination of the academic achievement gap that exists between a child with a disability and his same-age, typical peers. Arguably this statement dispels a widely-held understanding that the elimination of this gap is the universal goal of special education.

To receive special education services a student must meet a two-part eligibility criterion: satisfy the criteria that have been established for one or more of the categories of disability that are listed in the IDEA and, due to the manifestation of the disability, function or perform in a way that warrants special education services.

The IDEA's general least restrictive environment requirement establishes the general education classroom as the default location where a child with a disability is to be educated to the maximum extent appropriate.

Special education services can be configured so that a student with a disability receives the intensive intervention that is a part of an RTI framework. Conversely a student with a disability can be removed from the framework if too much of an emphasis is placed on the use of supplementary aids, services, and supports to enable the student to be physically present in a general education classroom.

SPECIAL EDUCATION AND AN RTI FRAMEWORK

The content that is presented in this chapter is intended to provide you with a fundamental understanding of the aim of special education plus an explanation of how special education interfaces with the other elements of an RTI framework. In particular, emphasis is placed on the care that must be taken to design and implement special education services in ways that complement the high quality and intense instruction that is available through a response-to-intervention framework rather than replace some of these needed services (especially when these services directly address the instructional needs of students with disabilities).

First, two foundational elements of special education are explained. One element captures the overall intent of special education, which is to provide every student with a disability access and opportunity to a public-school education, while the other sets straight a common myth about the expected impact of special education. Further, the point is made that special education allows for a process that leads to the provision of services rather than a guaranteed outcome.

Second, two of the lessons learned from the initial efforts to implement special education are discussed with respect to the subsequent creation of an RTI framework. One lesson was recognizing the importance of the core curriculum to all students. The second lesson was having to find a way to provide needed services to all students who demonstrate persistent learning deficits—both those with and without identifiable disabilities. This effort has been referred to as "eliminating the instructional crack."

Third, the nature of special education is explored in some detail. This is done by (a) examining the definition for the term special education as it is put forth in the IDEA and (b) discussing how supplementary aids, services, and supports can either complement or undercut the high quality, intense instruction that is available in the framework. This exploration is done in a way that ties it to the key elements of the framework and its focus on satisfactory student progress in the core curriculum.

BRIEF INTRODUCTION TO TIER 3 SERVICES

Tier 3 pertains to special education programming which is, in and of itself, a very complex endeavor. Hence, simultaneously dealing with the nuances of special education programming as well as the nuances of a response-to-intervention framework presents a noteworthy challenge for school personnel.

Mindful of the fact that the overall intent of this book is to provide you with a comprehensive, yet fundamental, explanation of an RTI framework, the content that is presented in this chapter does not delve deeply into these nuances. Instead, a number of matters that are central to the provision of special education services are explained and then are discussed in terms of their relevance to the framework.

Several times in chapter 4 a point that was emphasized is that Tier 2 services are not to be "more of the same" Tier 1 services that have proven not to be as effective as hoped for with respect to students' attainment of targeted learning outcomes. Moreover, it was noted that students who receive Tier 2 services will continue to receive Tier 1 services. This predicament means that Tier 2 services have to be calculated to interface with Tier 1 services.

Likewise, Tier 3 services are to be distinct from Tier 1 and Tier 2 services yet calculated to interface with both. Calculating how these services will interface is critically important since it is possible to provide a student with a disability who receives special education services less intense services, overall, than was the case when he was being provided Tier 1 and Tier 2 services. This can occur when emphasis is misplaced on the way that services are provided so that the student can remain, almost exclusively, in the general education classroom per the IDEA's general least restrictive environment requirement and its designation of the general education classroom as the default location where the student is to be educated.

In these instances, the student is provided special education services in the form of accommodations or scaffolds rather than the intense, remedial instruction he actually needs. In many situations, available resources allow schools to adequately support one situation but not both at the same time.

THE MANY FACETS OF SPECIAL EDUCATION

An appropriate starting point for discussing special education in the context of a response-to-intervention framework is to examine what could be characterized as some of the components of the foundation of special education. In this section three of these components are highlighted.

Special Education as Access and Opportunity

The original version of what was to become the IDEA, the Education for All Handicapped Children Act[1] that was passed in 1974, was crafted to provide students with disabilities access and opportunity with respect to a public education. The EAHCA was passed at a point in time when some students with disabilities were not permitted to attend a public school. Because it was

reasoned that these students—who demonstrated significant intellectual disabilities—were not capable of learning, they were not allowed to attend
school. The EAHCA sought to remedy this circumstance.[2,3]

Further it was argued by proponents of the legislation that other students
with specific learning disabilities were in public schools but were not being
provided the services they needed to give them an opportunity to attain the
learning outcomes that were associated with the general education curriculum. The EAHCA addressed this matter as well.

Special Education is a Process

These two distinct scenarios described above shed light on the complex
nature of the design and implementation of special education services.
Contrary to popular belief, special education services are not, in every single
instance, intended to be provided to erase the academic achievement differences that exist between the students who receive these services and those
who do not. In other words, the sole focus of special education is not necessarily to eliminate the gaps that may exist in the attainment of targeted
learning outcomes by the students who receive these services and those who
do not.

Rather, instead of thinking that the provision of special education services
is designed to lead a student to a pre-determined outcome, such as the awarding of a standard high school diploma, special education should be thought of
as allowing for a process that includes (a) conducting evaluations to determine which students have disabilities and are in need of special education
services, (b) identifying learning outcomes that are appropriate for these
students to work to attain, and (c) providing general and special education
services in ways that are believed to be necessary to enable a student to attain
the outcomes.

This process allows special education to be many things for many students. This aspect of special education is realized through the development of
what is called an individualized education plan (IEP) for each student with a
disability.

For a student with a specific learning disability that adversely affects his
attainment of basic reading skills, his special education services might consist of specialized instruction that results in him acquiring these skills and
subsequently progressing through the core curriculum such that he is
awarded a standard high school diploma.

For a student with an intellectual disability that is characterized as significant and results in noteworthy challenges mastering basic academic skills
(e.g., counting to ten and writing one's name) as well as independently
performing activities of daily living (e.g., getting dressed, preparing a meal),
special education services might consist of instruction intended to teach the

student these types of skills but only in the context of receiving supports concurrently from an adult. This arrangement is settled upon because those who design and implement this student's school program recognize that he will need support from others throughout his entire life.

Yet, the diverse nature of special education is intended to ensure that the purpose of the IDEA, which has also been referred to as its mission statement, is realized by every student with a disability. The IDEA's purpose is to prepare students with disabilities for further education, employment, and independent living during their post-secondary years.

This discussion of special education as a process that leads to the provision of needed services addresses an often-heard misstatement by school personnel who say that a student with a disability "has been placed in special education." Arguably this statement causes one to think that the term special education refers to a location where a wholly separate set of rules and procedures have been established for the purpose of educating the student. This scenario is analogous to saying that someone has been put in the hospital. This statement clearly refers to a location that is separate from the mainstream of society, is governed by some unique rules, and in which specialized services are provided.

The placement, meaning location, where a student with a disability is provided educational services is a topic worthy of discussion in its own right. In fact, it is a very important topic. However, it is one of a number of important topics that, considered altogether, result in what is referred to as an appropriate education for a student with a disability.

An examination of these foundational issues highlights one major difference between special education and an RTI framework. Whereas the focus of the special education process is an individualized education plan for each student, the principal focus of the heart of the framework—its Tier 1 and Tier 2 services—is each student's satisfactory progress in the core curriculum through instruction that, ultimately and exclusively, is presented in the general education classroom.

SPECIAL EDUCATION AND THE EVOLUTION OF THE RESPONSE-TO-INTERVENTION FRAMEWORK

During the first twenty-five years when the federal special education legislation was implemented a number of important lessons were learned from some of the outcomes that were realized. Two of the outcomes involved the types of programs students were being provided and which students were receiving needed remedial services—special education or otherwise. The lessons that were learned from these two outcomes led, in part, to the creation of the framework.

Two-Track Educational System

One outcome that resulted from the initial efforts at implementing special education programs was what was referred to as a two-track educational system within public schools.[4,5] One of the tracks was designed and implemented for students who were not determined to be eligible to receive special education services. These students were expected to master, or acquire, the content that, today, would comprise the core curriculum. The other track was the one that, on a student-by-student basis, was designed and implemented on behalf of children with disabilities—otherwise known as children determined to be eligible to receive special education services.

The connection of these students to the core curriculum often was not easy to determine and in a number of instances little or no effort was made to teach these students traditional academic content, such as age-appropriate, grade-level reading and math. Rather, these students were taught what are referred to as either life skills or activities of daily living, which included tasks such as how to make their bed, clean dishes, shop for groceries, make a sandwich or do a load of laundry.

The existence of this second track raised a number of concerns. One of the primary concerns were the limitations that would be realized by students who had not been given an opportunity to learn traditional academic content that, based upon its inclusion in the core curriculum, had been determined to be important for post-high school education, employment, and independent living.

In particular, a student who had not been taught this curriculum certainly would not be prepared to pursue a college degree. This was very much a concern for the majority of students who had been identified as being eligible to receive special education services as a result of a specific learning disability that was based upon the presence of average to above average intelligence but noteworthy difficulties learning how to read.

This lesson led to a renewed emphasis for all students to learn the content that comprises the core curriculum. Since this curriculum is the focus of the instruction that is presented in general education classrooms, a renewed emphasis also was placed on keeping students with disabilities in these classrooms. The response-to-intervention framework emerged as one way to address both of these matters.

Concerns About How to Address the Needs of Students with Learning Challenges

As has been noted previously, research associated with the implementation of special education has documented the difficulty in distinguishing between the academic performances of some students with specific learning disabilities and students with slightly below average intelligence and concomitant levels of academic achievement. Hence, one of the driving forces behind the advocacy for the use of a response-to-intervention framework is a concern about how best to address the challenge schools face to simultaneously provide needed services to both groups of students.

Prior to the push for the implementation of the framework it was common for students with specific learning disabilities to receive additional services beyond those that were available in the general education classroom while the other low achieving students did not receive any additional services. These students were said to be "falling through an instructional crack," which meant that there was a gap between the general education services they were being provided and the remedial services they needed, and that needed to be systematically attached to the general education services to eliminate the gap.

Two other related concerns emerged. One was the noteworthy costs for special education services. These costs can be two to three times the cost of providing educational services to students who receive instruction exclusively in general education classrooms. The framework's Tier 2 services were conceptualized as one way to reduce the costs of special education by preventing some students from having to receive these services.

Another concern was the legal requirement to exclude inadequate instruction as a primary reason for the lack of academic achievement by a student with a specific learning disability. Providing intense interventions in Tier 2 as a supplement to high quality Tier 1 instruction added validity to a special education eligibility determination team's conclusion that a student's lack of achievement was the result of an innate disability rather than an extraneous factor such as inadequate instruction.

A DEEPER UNDERSTANDING OF SPECIAL EDUCATION AND ITS RELATIONSHIP TO AN RTI FRAMEWORK

Designing and implementing appropriate special education services is a complex endeavor for no other reason than these services must be based on the unique needs of a particular student with a disability. In the IDEA this concept is called individualized instruction (which is separate from providing a student instruction using a 1:1 pupil teacher ratio). Given the fact that no two students are exactly the same, no two sets of special education services will be exactly the same.

Another reason why providing special education services is a complex endeavor is that these services must interface with other instructional services that are being presented. When a response-to-intervention framework is not being employed in a school, special education services must be designed to interface with the services that are being provided in a general education classroom. Yet, when the framework is being employed special education services must interface with both Tier 1 and Tier 2 services.

This interfacing cannot be more of the same instruction. However, a unique situation arises when a response-to-intervention framework is being used in a school because Tier 2 intense intervention—particularly ultra-intense Tier 2 intervention—can be subverted via the provision of certain types of special education services.

Hence, the purpose of this section is to explain special education in detail so that you can consider it within the context of an RTI framework in a way that enables a student to profit from the effective services that are available from both special education and the framework.

Special Education Defined

Special education is defined in the IDEA as "specially designed instruction to meet the unique needs of a child with a disability." A fundamental understanding of special education, and the outcome a student might realize if special education services are provided, can be gained by analyzing the various components of the definition.

Within the definition for special education is the phrase "specially designed instruction,"[6] which refers to three aspects of the instruction that is presented to a child with a disability: content, methodology, and delivery of instruction. When special education services are provided one or more of these aspects of instruction has to be addressed so that the instruction that is presented to a child with a disability is markedly different from the instruction that is provided to same-age peers in the general education classroom.

For instance, a sixth-grade student who is receiving special education services to address his subpar performance in reading may be taught second grade, rather than sixth grade, reading content since the second-grade content serves as a foundation for higher level reading skills and is at the student's instructional level. Regarding the uses of methodologies that might be considered to be special education, teachers may use American Sign Language as one method for communicating with a student who is deaf or Braille as one way of communicating with a student who is blind.

Furthermore, the definition for special education states that it is to "meet the unique needs" of a child with a disability. Essentially this refers to the fact that the services that are provided to a child must be based on an examination of the child's distinct instructional needs more so than the child's particular disability. In other words, schools cannot simply offer a generic autism program for students with this disability. At one point in time this is what happened with respect to students with a specific learning disability.

Shortly after the first version of the IDEA was passed, some schools established generic specific learning disabilities programs and simply placed every child who was identified as having a specific learning disability in that program where they were taught the exact same content via the exact same methodology. This arrangement could not adequately address the instructional needs that manifest as a result of this disability, which include academic achievement deficits in one or more of seven areas: basic reading skills, reading comprehension, math calculation, math reasoning, written expression, oral expression, and listening comprehension.

By one estimate, the students who share the same disability classification—specific learning disability—can exhibit up to 500,000 unique learning challenges.[7] This means that one child with a specific learning disability may demonstrate challenges learning basic reading skills, another math calculation skills, and still another basic reading, reading comprehension, and oral expression skills. The unique needs of each of these students are to be addressed through the provision of special education services.

The last part of the definition for special education—"child with a disability"—refers to a student, ages three to twenty-one, inclusive, who has been found to meet the eligibility criteria for the receipt of special education services. These criteria are discussed in more detail below.

In this section the points that are to be made are that, at a minimum, special education services are to be provided beginning the day an eligible child turns three years of age through the last day they are twenty-one. Furthermore, while the phrase "child with a disability" is used throughout the IDEA it has been established that this phrase refers to all students who have been determined to be eligible to receive special education services, which would include middle and high school students who would be referred to more commonly as young adults rather than children.

Two-Part Special Education Eligibility Criteria

To be eligible for the receipt of special education services a child must meet the two-part eligibility criteria that have been established by the IDEA.[8] The first criterion is that a child must meet the criteria that have been established for one or more of the categories of disability that are listed in the IDEA. For instance, in order to be identified as having an intellectual disability a child must meet the following four criteria. It must demonstrate significantly subaverage intellectual functioning that exists concurrently with substandard academic achievement and impairs the performance of functional tasks while manifesting during the developmental period.

The second criterion is that a determination must be made that because of the manifestation of the child's disability he needs to be provided special education services (i.e., the specially designed instruction explained above).

For example, if a child's intellectual disability results in a child who is in the fifth grade having only mastered early first grade math skills, then the child may be determined to be eligible to receive special education services to address the student's need for specially designed instruction in math. In this instance, the child's specially designed instruction would involve teaching the child math content that is at the child's instructional level (i.e., first grade), which is markedly different from the fifth-grade content that is being taught to his same-age, typical peers.

The two-part eligibility criteria can result in situations in which a child meets the criteria for one or more of the IDEA's categories of disability, but the disability does not manifest in a way that causes the child to need special education. There are reported instances where the child has met the criteria for an intellectual disability, or mental retardation, but is not functioning much differently from the majority of same age peers who also are functioning at a level that is much lower than established chronological age/grade-level standards.

Highlighting the two-part eligibility criteria for the provision of special education services brings light to one of the many complexities that are involved in the implementation of an RTI framework. That is to say that in some instances a child will not be determined to be eligible to receive special education services even though the child has a disability that could qualify him to receive these services. The resulting question school personnel will have to address is how Tier 2 services will be configured so as to be able to address these circumstances.

One way is to continue them indefinitely as ultra-intense interventions while another is to permit a student to enter and exit Tier 2 on an "as needed" basis. This is one example of how special education interfaces with the components of the framework. In this instance the special education eligibility determination process results in a determination that a student is not eligible for special education services but still needs services beyond those provided in Tier 1.

The General Education Classroom as Both the Default Placement and a Part of Intense Intervention in a Response-to-Intervention Framework

To garner a full understanding of how special education services interface with the other components of the framework, you must be knowledgeable of the IDEA's emphasis on children with disabilities being educated in the general education classroom using the general education curriculum "to the maximum extent appropriate." In the IDEA what is termed the general least restrictive environment requirement directs, or sets guidelines for, deciding upon the location where a child with a disability is to be educated. In accordance with this requirement, the general education classroom is the default placement.

However, factors such as the curriculum that is taught (traditional academic content versus functional tasks, or activities of daily living) and a student's displays of disruptive behavior can serve as the basis for deciding that a student should be placed, or educated, in a setting other than the general education classroom. These settings include, but are not limited to, resource rooms, self-contained classrooms, homes, and hospitals.

In the vast-majority of instances adherence to the general least restrictive environment requirement means that once a child with a disability is determined to be eligible to receive special education services this eligibility will place a renewed emphasis on an examination of the services the child will receive in the general education classroom. This circumstance is one reason why, previously, the point was emphasized that a child is not placed in special education. Rather, a child is determined to be eligible to receive special education services and, in most instances, these services will be provided in a general education classroom.

With respect to a response-to-intervention framework the challenge for school personnel will be how to interface the special education services with the Tier 1 services in a general education classroom. A key issue that will need to be addressed is how to balance the need to keep a child with a disability in the general education classroom as much as possible against providing the child with needed intensive intervention.

What could happen is that, in a well-meaning attempt to keep the child in the general education classroom, too much of an emphasis can be put on physically having the child in this location at the expense of providing the child with much needed remedial instruction. This phenomenon has been described as special education accommodations as opposed to intense instruction.

The reason intense intervention can be de-emphasized is because the child will be provided with what are known as supplementary aids, services, and supports for the purpose of enabling the child to attain targeted learning outcomes in the general education classroom and curriculum. These aids, services, and supports are wide ranging, as the list below indicates:[9]

1. Support and training for staff
2. Planning time for staff collaboration
3. Assignment modifications (e.g., shorter assignments, relatively long assignments broken into "chunks")
4. Environmental supports (e.g., preferential seating; planned seating on the bus, in the classroom, and at lunch; altered room arrangement)
5. Specialized equipment needs (e.g., wheelchair, augmentative communication device, restroom equipment)

6. Pacing of instruction (e.g., breaks, extended time)
7. Material needs (e.g., advanced copies of teacher's notes, large print or Braille)
8. Testing adaptations (e.g., read test to child, extend time)

The challenge is to not allow special education services to result in a student essentially being removed from a response-to-intervention framework. In other words, if

1. supplementary aids, services, and supports,
2. accommodations, and
3. modifications

are provided in a way to enable a student to remain in a general education classroom without the student simultaneously being provided intense small group or 1:1 instruction that addresses his individualized needs (i.e., academic content that is not being addressed in the general education classroom), then the student would no longer be included in the framework as it is described.

The bottom line is that we want students to be successful in the general education classroom and curriculum. The question that must be answered adequately is how to go about making this happen with the use of all of the services in the framework—which includes special education services.

Why Differentiate Between RTI and Special Education Services

It is logical to conclude that if it is difficult to differentiate between the performance of students with specific learning disabilities and their peers with low average intelligence and concomitant academic achievement then, likewise, it will be difficult to distinguish between their instructional needs. In fact, in a number of instances both groups of students require very similar services. Thus, it is fair to ask why there is a need to go through the special education eligibility process.

One reason why the special education eligibility process must be followed is because it is mandated by federal law. As a condition of one's employment in a public school a teacher—and every other employee—is obligated to adhere to the stipulations in the IDEA and its accompanying regulations.

A second, and closely related, reason for going through the special education eligibility process is that the services that are settled upon are guaranteed to be provided. On the other hand, similar services that are available through an RTI framework, such as Tier 2 services, come with no such guarantee.

Instead these services are provided because of a well-founded belief that they will result in effective instruction for the students who receive them.

Special Education Eligibility: The End of the Beginning

As is noted several times in this book, a central argument in favor or in support of the framework is that its implementation satisfies certain requirements in the IDEA for the identification of children with disabilities, particularly those who are being evaluated to determine whether they are eligible to receive special education services as the result of a specific learning disability. While the eligibility determination process is arduous, the work that is performed in this process is not a means to an end. Rather, it is the end of the beginning. Eligibility determination is the first step among many that are taken to ensure a child with a disability is provided a free and appropriate public education.

Accordingly, listed below are the four factors that must be addressed when determining whether an appropriate education under the IDEA has been provided:

1. Was the program individualized on the basis of the student's assessment and performance?
2. Was the program delivered in the least restrictive environment?
3. Were the services provided in a coordinated and collaborative manner by key stakeholders?
4. Were positive academic and nonacademic benefits demonstrated?

CHAPTER 5 COMPREHENSION CHECK

Now that you have finished reading the chapter, you should be able to:

- Explain what is meant by the following statement: "Special education was originally designed to provide students with disabilities access and opportunity."
- Discuss how the existence of a two-track educational system led to today's focus on teaching all students with disabilities some form of the core curriculum.
- Explain the difference between special education as intensive intervention and special education as accommodations.
- Discuss the general least restrictive environment requirement that is put forth in the IDEA.
- Explain what is meant by the following statement: "A student is determined to be eligible to receive special education services as opposed to having been placed in special education."

- Describe the two-part special education eligibility criterion.
- List and explain the three components of the definition for the term "special education" that is put forth in the IDEA.
- Differentiate between an instructional accommodation and an instructional modification.
- List three examples of supplementary aids, services, and supports.

NOTES

1. Education for All Handicapped Children Act, Pub. L No. 94–142, (1975).

2. Mitchell L. Yell and David F. Bateman, "Endrew F. v. Douglas County School District (2017) FAPE and the US Supreme Court," *TEACHING Exceptional Children* 50, no. 1 (2017): 7–15.

3. Angela M. T. Prince, Mitchell L. Yell, and Antonis Katsiyannis, "Endrew F. v. Douglas County School District (2017): The US Supreme Court and Special Education," *Intervention in School and Clinic* 53, no. 5 (2018): 321–324.

4. M. L. Anderegg and Glenn A. Vergason, "An Analysis of One of the Cornerstones of the Regular Education Initiative," *Focus on Exceptional Children* 20, no. 8 (1988): 1–7.

5. The Regular Education Initiative: A Statement by the Teacher Education Division, Council for Exceptional Children October 1986, *Journal of Learning Disabilities* 20, no. 5 (1987): 289–293, https://doi.org/10.1177/002221948702000508.

6. Mitchell L. Yell, *The Law and Special Education*, third edition, ed. Jeffrey Johnston, (Upper Saddle River, NJ: Pearson Education, Inc. 2012).

7. Cecil D. Mercer and Ann R. Mercer, *Students with Learning Disabilities*, third edition. (Merrill, 1997), ISBN: 9780134771762.

8. H. Rutherford Turnbull III and Ann P. Turnbull, *Free Appropriate Public Education: The Law and Children with Disabilities* (Denver: Love Publishing Company).

9. U.S. Department of Education, "Supplementary Aids and Services," Center for Parent Information and Resources. Last modified November 2017, https://www.parentcenterhub.org/iep-supplementary/.

Chapter Six

Assessment

OVERVIEW

In this chapter you will learn about the assessment component of a response-to-intervention framework as well as relevant information about the global topic of educational assessment. Key points from the chapter include the following:

One primary component of an RTI framework is an assessment component. It consists of screeners to identify students who are at-risk for attaining targeted learning outcomes and progress monitoring to assess each student's advancement in the core curriculum.

The terms assessment, testing, and evaluation are often used interchangeably but actually have distinct meanings. Assessment is defined as the collection of information while testing refers to the means by which the presence of something, such as a student's mastery of targeted learning outcomes, is determined. Evaluation involves placing a value judgement on information obtained via assessment.

Assessment can either inform instruction or act as a barrier. When assessment informs instruction, the teacher uses the information to decide whether and how she will adjust her instruction. When assessment acts as a barrier, the information is used to apply consequences, such as identifying which students will be awarded a standard high school diploma.

A high stakes test is one that involves the application of important consequences. When high stakes tests are administered schools must make students aware of a number of relevant matters, including the content that will be tested and the consequences for passing or failing the test.

The items that comprise an RTI framework's assessment component are but one part of a school's assessment milieu. Other assessments schools' conduct includes those used to assign grades, high stakes tests, and assessments required for special education programming.

Relevant educational assessment terms and topics include whether there are prescribed ways to conduct a particular assessment (formal/informal), the frequency with which assessment is conducted (formative/summative), and the standards that are used to evaluate a student's performance on an assessment (criterion/norm-referenced).

Testing accommodations are changes to the conditions under which an assessment is conducted and are intended to ensure the validity of the results that are obtained. Accommodations may involve the amount of time a student is given to complete an assessment, how the test items are presented, the student's mode of responding, and the setting where the assessment is conducted.

A FOCUS ON A CONCEPTUAL
UNDERSTANDING OF ASSESSMENT

Chapter 1 noted that an RTI framework is comprised of two essential elements: an assessment component and a tiered intervention component. Chapters 1-5 explained the tiered intervention component. In this chapter basic information about the assessment component and related issues is presented.

The focus of this chapter is the information that you, particularly a beginning teacher, need to know about assessment as it relates to, or is addressed in, the framework. The assessment component of the framework consists of (a) a universal screener that is conducted to determine the students for whom there is a relatively high probability that they will not attain expected learning outcomes after receiving only Tier 1 intervention services and (b) ongoing progress monitoring to assess each student's advancement in the core curriculum.

Yet, there is also a third type of assessment that stems from the framework. This involves the assessment that is part of the evaluation that is conducted to determine whether a student meets the eligibility criteria for special education services.

In this chapter, both information about the framework's assessment component and basic concepts about assessment are discussed as opposed to intricate details about the design and administration of what are commonly referred to as assessment instruments. Additionally, the ways in which assessment is directly related to effective, high quality instruction are discussed. This discussion centers on how the data that are obtained from assessments can guide you in presenting instruction. Another way of saying this is that you will learn how assessment informs instruction.

Regarding assessment instruments, you may think of these as the actual tests you will administer to students. Each test either specifies who is qualified to administer it based upon their prior training and current credentials (e.g., a board licensed psychologist) or who can become qualified to administer it (e.g., a special education teacher who receives training from a certified teacher who has at least two years experience administering the test).

In most instances a school district or an individual school will select the assessment instruments they will use, determine the training requirements for those who will administer the tests, and then ensure that the training is provided. Therefore, it is important that you have a conceptual understanding of assessment and the framework rather than detailed knowledge about particular assessment instruments or topics. You will acquire this information at the time you need to do so as well as in the school where you need to do so.

KEY TERMS: ASSESSMENT, TESTING, AND EVALUATION

Oftentimes the terms "assessment," "test," and "evaluation" are used interchangeably, as if they were synonymous. Although their meanings are related in that they pertain to information about students' performances in terms of their attainment of academic knowledge and skills and school social behaviors, their meanings are distinct. Understanding the different definitions for these terms will further your understanding of an RTI framework's assessment component.

"Assessment" is defined as the collection of information. One type of assessment is informal assessment, which refers to the collection of information that is not governed by established procedures. Some of these types of assessment occur without the teacher giving much thought about the fact that she is conducting this type of assessment. Yet, the data (i.e., information) she collects readily informs her instruction.

For example, a teacher may observe that when she seats two students next to each other they engage in more instances of disruptive behavior than when they are seated far apart. Consequently, she accounts for this when she arranges her classroom seating chart so as to produce a safe and orderly environment that sets the stage for effective instruction.

Likewise, she might observe a student who quickly becomes frustrated when he does not know how to complete an assignment. When he becomes frustrated he just sits quietly at his desk but wastes valuable academic learning time. In response to this behavior the teacher adjusts her routine so that after she gives her class a task to perform she follows up with this student shortly afterward to provide needed support. She also allows for him to ask a nearby peer, who typically knows what to do, for assistance if she is not available.

Testing is the means by which the presence of something is determined. In schools, tests determine the presence of things such as a student's academic knowledge and skills or his ability to perform a social behavior.

Mostly a test consists of the presentation of a stimulus, or some type of directive, to which a student must provide a response independently. Examples include a teacher presenting (a) the directive, "Spell the word coat;" (b) the written instruction, "Compare and contrast Nakisha and JaQuan's reactions to the loss of their beloved pet dog," on an English test; or (c) "Simplify 2x + 6x -4" on an Algebra test.

When most people refer to taking a test, they are describing a situation during which a student, sitting at her desk with a pencil in hand, makes independent responses to questions or similar items, such as task directives, that are posed. In other words, a student is required to demonstrate her knowledge or skill in response to a task directive. The student's responses provide information, which is assessment. When a grade is assigned this is evaluation.

Evaluation refers to placing a value on the merits, or meaning, of the information, or data, obtained via assessment. For example, a student who answers 65 percent of the questions correctly on a final exam may have his performance characterized as satisfactory while a classmate who answers 97 percent of the questions correctly has her performance characterized as superior.

A REVIEW OF THE RESPONSE-TO-INTERVENTION FRAMEWORK'S ASSESSMENT COMPONENT

In an RTI framework the overarching purpose of the assessment component is to ensure that students are placed in the tiers that allow for the services the students need. [1,2] To achieve this purpose two types of formal assessment are conducted: screening and student progress monitoring. Each is reviewed briefly below.

Screening

Screening refers to an assessment that is intended to sort out, from a large population of individuals, a smaller number who need to be examined further in accordance with the focus of the screening. Consider an examination to determine whether an individual needs to be prescribed eyeglasses. This examination likely begins with the administration of a well-known screener for visual acuity: the Snellen eye chart.

A relatively small number of individuals' performances on this screening will be interpreted to mean that they must undergo a more in-depth examination for the purpose of determining the precise status of their visual acuity and an appropriate treatment (e.g., nearsightedness treated with a prescription for eyeglasses).

In the framework the purpose of a screener is to predict which students will not achieve expected learning outcomes if they continue in their current Tier 1 program, such as mastering end of the year benchmarks in reading and math. It is a type of assessment characterized by quick, low cost, repeatable testing of age-appropriate skills (e.g., identifying letters of the alphabet or reading a list of high-frequency words) or school social behaviors (e.g., tardiness, aggression, or hyperactivity). In the framework, screening is to be conducted two to three times per year.

Hence, a screener's predictive validity is one of its most important features. Predictive validity refers to the extent that a screener accurately identifies students who would not have attained targeted learning outcomes had they received only Tier 1 services. Furthermore, sensitivity is a screening measure's ability to identify "true positives" (i.e., those students who perform poorly on a reading screener and end up having problems learning how to read) whereas specificity refers to a screening measure's ability to identify "true negatives" (i.e., those students who do not perform poorly on the screen and do not end up demonstrating reading problems).[3]

Factors that can affect a screening measure's sensitivity and specificity include whether the measure is criterion- or norm-referenced, and what cut scores distinguish levels of performance. A cut score is the point that represents the dividing line between students who are not at risk and those assumed to be. These students are sorted out from the larger population of their peers and are examined further or immediately provided Tier 2 services.

School Criteria for Determining Which Students Receive Tier 2 Services Based on Screening Data

As soon as screening data are obtained they should be evaluated to determine which students need to be provided Tier 2 services. Below are some examples of criteria that have been established for the purpose of identifying students who would be considered to be at-risk for attaining targeted learning outcomes solely from being provided Tier 1 services.

Administer a screening instrument that has an established benchmark with predictive validity regarding students' end of the year performance with respect to measures of their attainment of targeted learning outcomes

Examine students' performances on the previous year's high stakes test and select a criterion (e.g., the bottom 25 percent of scores) that identifies these students;

Based on the results obtained from a norm referenced assessment identify any student who scores below the 25th percentile;

Use a criterion referenced measure and establish a performance benchmark that, if a student scores below it, will identify him as at-risk.[4]

Student Progress Monitoring

Broadly stated, student progress monitoring involves an assessment of all of
the skills that a student is to learn during the school year.[5] Like other assessment data it is used to evaluate a teacher's instructional effectiveness and to
inform instruction.

Progress monitoring assessments address all of the skills a student must
master and not just the skills that are covered in the current unit of instruction. Additionally, they are conducted to determine a student's level and rate
of learning.

The initial assessment identifies a student's level of attainment of the
targeted learning outcomes, and from the data obtained a calculation is made
about the rate of learning a student must demonstrate over the course of the
school year in order to master all of the targeted learning outcomes. Students
whose rate of learning falls a certain percentage (e.g., 20 percent) or more
below what is needed to meet the end of the year outcomes would be identified as being in need of instruction beyond what is being provided in Tier 1
in the general education classroom.

Progress Monitoring Data Informing High Quality Instruction

Teachers can use progress monitoring data to initiate a detailed examination
of their presentation of high-quality instruction. This examination should
include an analysis of how each feature of high-quality instruction is either
contributing to, or detracting from, a student's progress. This circumstance
highlights the need to operationally define high quality instruction. Doing so
provides teachers with a mechanism for objectively assessing the overall
effectiveness of their instruction.

RATIONALE FOR ASSESSMENT:
INFORMING INSTRUCTION OR ACTING AS A BARRIER

There are two basic purposes of assessment, which can exist separately or in
combination. One purpose is to inform instruction while the other is to serve
as a barrier, or function as a gatekeeper, in terms of the outcomes some entity
(student, teacher, or school) does or does not receive based on the results of
an assessment. Most of the discussion in the previous section highlighted
how the assessments in a response-to-intervention framework's assessment
component inform instruction. In this section, that aspect of assessment is

reviewed briefly and is followed by an explanation of how assessment can act as a barrier. Within this explanation high stakes testing is discussed.

When assessment informs instruction, it means that the assessment data are used by the teacher when she makes decisions about how to present instruction differently from how she previously did with the expectation that the new way will be more effective and efficient. Assessments can inform instruction in one of two ways. One way is by providing information about students' behaviors. The other way is providing information about the teacher's behavior.

When assessment serves as a barrier, or gate keeper, it means that the data are used to determine whether either an advantageous or adverse consequence—for either a student, teacher, or a school—will be applied. Examples for a student would be promotion to the next grade versus retention in the current grade, and the awarding, or not, of a standard high school diploma. An example for a school might be receiving a designation that would allow for financial rewards to be paid to the staff versus the reassignment or removal of administrators and other staff. Discussions about assessment serving as a barrier must simultaneously involve discussions about what has been characterized as high stakes testing.

High stakes testing refers to testing that has noteworthy consequences for one or more stakeholders, which includes individual students, teachers, and administrators, or even the entire school. There are a number of stipulations that have to be addressed when high stakes tests are used, and these stipulations have a direct impact on both teachers and students.

First, students must be told they will be tested. Second, they must be told the content, or curriculum, that will be tested. Third, they must be told the outcome for passing or failing to pass the test as well as the criteria for passing or failing. Fourth, they must be taught the content tested. Fifth, the tests that are administered must be valid and reliable for their stated purpose.

High stakes testing will be an issue in a response-to-intervention framework when the work performed in it is related, in some way, to a high stakes test. This may be the case when a student who receives Tier 3 services as the result of a language impairment must pass both a high school English class as well as a mandated state test to meet two of the many requirements that have been set forth to earn a standard high school diploma.

While it is important for you to be aware of the many issues that pertain to the assessment of students, the primary focus on assessment within an RTI framework and your role as a teacher is as a tool to inform instruction. Thus, in the next section information is presented about the relative standing of assessment activities to the other instructional tasks' teachers need to attend to.

RTI'S ASSESSMENT COMPONENT:
ONE PART OF THE ASSESSMENT MILIEU

Once one understands the nuances between terms that pertain to students' mastery of expected learning outcomes—such as assessment, testing, and evaluation—one can appreciate how much assessment takes place every day within a school. This understanding highlights the fact that the framework's assessment component will be one part of a school's assessment milieu. In other words, this component will not be the school's exclusive assessment activity.

Hence, one goal of this chapter is to provide a satisfactory explanation of the framework's assessment component while simultaneously explaining how it fits within the larger context of all of a school's assessment activities. In the end, the challenge for schools will be (a) determining how much, and what kind, of data to collect and then (b) to use the weight of the evidence, or data, that they have collected to match the available instructional services to each student's instructional needs.

Total Time for Assessment

Viewing assessment as a tool for informing instruction allows one to guard against assessment taking on a bigger role than it should. Consider the following experience of a high school teacher who was assigned to teach a semester-long Algebra 1 course. The course met five days a week, ninety-four minutes each day, for eighteen weeks. This meant that 120 days were allocated to this course.

The time for the formal assessments that were conducted in this course was as follows:

1. Two days for the state mandated test (A student was required to earn a passing score on this test in order to meet one requirement for earning a standard high school diploma.)
2. Four days for a district mandated test that had been designed to (a) provide the students with an experience that would be similar to the state mandated test that they would take and (b) provide the district with data that predicted how the student would perform on the state-mandated test
3. Two days for a mid-semester exam and a final exam, and eight days for end of unit tests

This arrangement resulted in the students spending approximately 13 percent of the allocated time engaged in formal assessment activities. Yet, the percentage of time that some students spent in assessment activities was far greater. A number of students with disabilities were, in accordance with their IEP, provided with an accommodation that permitted them to have extra time to complete each test. Also, during the class periods when a test was administered, all of the students were given the entire period to complete the test even though the majority did finish the test with plenty of allocated time remaining.

The teacher did use the information to inform her instruction. However, her ultimate goal was to have each student pass the state test. A student could earn a passing score on this test by earning just over 30 percent of all of the points possible. Not surprisingly, a number of students who earned this passing score were observed to be struggling in their next math class, which built upon the skills they were to have mastered in the Algebra 1 class.

In this instance it is fair, some would argue absolutely necessary, to ask if more instruction and less assessment would have resulted in the same or even better student learning outcomes. This story highlights the need to analyze the role of assessment relative to the merits of presenting instruction, especially instruction that counts as academic learning time.

Summary of Ongoing School Assessment Activities

As was just noted, response-to-intervention assessments are not exclusive. Other assessments that are being conducted in a school include:

1. Informal assessments that readily inform daily instruction (e.g. anecdotal data)
2. Mastery measurements that are used to assign grades (e.g., end of unit or chapter tests, midterm and final exams, long term projects such as a term paper)
3. High stakes tests and related assessments (e.g., subject area tests and related predictive validity tests, such as the district mandated Algebra 1 test described above)
4. Assessments required for special education programming (e.g., functional behavioral assessments, eligibility determination evaluations)

A FEW MORE KEY ASSESSMENT TERMS AND CONCEPTS FOR A SCHOOL'S ASSESSMENT MILIEU

To round out your basic understanding of assessment, testing, and evaluation some additional topics are identified and explained below:

Formal versus Informal Assessment

The terms formal and informal assessment refer to whether there are specific, prescribed ways to conduct the assessment. Formal assessments are prescribed ways of finding out what a student has learned, or how much she has improved during an instructional period. These assessments have standardized methods of administration and grading. Examples of formal assessments include, but certainly are not limited to, intelligence tests, screeners and academic achievement tests. An assessment that is a part of an RTI framework's progress monitoring protocol is an example of a formal assessment.

Informal assessments refer to various ways of collecting data without the use of standardized, formal methods. Examples of these assessments are teacher observations, student's daily classwork, and pop quizzes. Informal assessments are what teachers use every day to evaluate their students' performance and progress. Thus, they immediately inform instruction.

Formative versus Summative Assessment

The terms formative and summative assessment refer to when, meaning how often, assessments are administered.

Formative assessments are administered often. Hence, you should think of the "f" in formative as also being the "f" in the word frequent.

Formative assessment is an integral part of Tier 2 and Tier 3 intervention services, with these assessments being administered as often as two or three times per week, or even daily. Formative assessments are generally low stakes and consist of probes. A probe is a short, easy to administer assessment that consists of a small number of items that are exclusively and directly tied to the content that is being addressed during instruction. Examples of probes include having a student read ten high frequency words, answer ten multiplication facts, and spell ten consonant-vowel-consonant words.

The goal of formative assessment is to monitor student learning by providing ongoing feedback that can be used by students to improve their learning and instructors to improve their teaching. Formative assessments help students identify their strengths and weaknesses and target areas that need work, and help instructors recognize where students are struggling and address problems immediately. Instructors can do this by revising the instructional strategies that have been used to teach skills students are not mastering or making progress towards mastering.

Summative assessments are administered periodically, most often following weeks of instruction. In most instances, the goal of a summative assessment is to evaluate student learning at the end of an instructional unit by comparing the student's performance against some standard or benchmark (i.e. curriculum objectives, learning outcomes, district grading scales) as well as a unit pre-test.

Examples of summative assessments include, but certainly are not limited to, final and mid-term exams and unit tests. Summative assessments also include high stakes tests.

Information from summative assessments can be used to inform instruction when students or instructors use it to guide their subsequent efforts and activities, such as when a teacher teaches a unit again in the future or immediately reteaches some or all of a unit based on the results from a summative assessment.

Criterion and Norm-Referenced Assessment

These terms criterion- and norm-referenced assessment address the standards that are used to evaluate a student's performance on an assessment. A criterion-referenced assessment compares a student's performance to a predetermined performance level on a targeted learning outcome, such as whether a student is able to name all twenty-six lowercase letters of the alphabet. Criterion-referenced assessments likely will be used when Tier 2 and Tier 3 intervention services are provided. A norm-referenced assessment compares a student's assessment results to an appropriate target group (e.g., other students the same grade), such as whether a student's score met or exceeded the scores of 75 percent or more of the students in his grade.

Quantitative, Qualitative, and Anecdotal Data

In chapter 3 you were introduced to the terms quantitative and qualitative in the context of research. In this context a quantitative study refers to research that gathered and analyzed empirical, or numerical data. Conclusions were drawn based on a mathematical analysis and concomitant interpretation of the data. A qualitative study describes data that are not mathematically derived. These studies report descriptions of observations and interactions, or ongoing events.

Quantitative and qualitative assessments have, relatively speaking, the same meanings as their similarly named research studies. Quantitative data is information about quantities; that is, information that can be measured and written down with numbers. Some examples of quantitative data are one's height and weight. Quantitative assessment involves data that are mathematically computed and summarized, such as scores for statistical significance.

Qualitative assessments generate descriptive, non-numerical information about things. This information pertains to features and attributes of a phenomenon, such as whether a person's outward disposition appears to be confident or bewildered. Since this type of information cannot actually be measured, qualitative assessments provide descriptions which tend not to be as precise as quantitative data.

Finally, anecdotal assessment essentially involves the telling of a story. Quite often teachers are encouraged to record anecdotal data which means they are to write a narrative in which they document the events they observed about a phenomenon of interest.

Level and Rate of Progress

Level of learning can be thought of as the amount or scope of a curriculum that a student has learned while rate of learning is how quickly the student learns new content. To the extent that a curriculum is vertically or horizontally sequenced, the level of learning refers to an arrangement where the learning of certain skills is to precede the learning of others. Thinking in terms of grade levels, at the end of the school year when a fourth-grade student shows, on an assessment, that he has mastered only first grade math skills, he would be said to be performing at a lower level than a classmate who has demonstrated mastery of the fourth-grade math skills.

The rate of learning refers to the ratio of the number of new skills learned per unit of time. For example, if twelve new skills were learned in six weeks then the rate of learning would be two skills per week (12 skills:6 weeks is 2 skills:1 week).

INSTRUCTIONAL VERSUS TESTING
ACCOMMODATION VERSUS MODIFICATION

Given the central role of assessment, testing, and evaluation in the present era of school accountability, a relevant topic of increasing significance is the use of testing accommodations. These are to be distinguished from instructional accommodations and modifications. As the terms imply, testing accommodations refer to times when you conduct assessments, particularly formal assessments that involve standardized tests, while instructional accommodations and modifications pertain to times when you are teaching.

Accommodations are changes to the conditions under which a student is expected to either learn or perform an academic skill or school social behavior, rather than an alteration (modification) of the standard that has been set for the performance of the task. The purpose for providing an accommodation is to ensure that a student's performance is a valid reflection of his ability to either learn or perform a targeted skill. Accommodations can address the following variables: time to complete a task, the manner in which the task is presented, a student's mode of responding, and setting arrangements.

Instructional Accommodations and Modifications

In terms of instruction, an accommodation involves a change to the conditions under which a student receives instruction. The purpose is to provide the student with conditions that enable him to use his abilities to learn rather than be hampered or prevented from doing so because of the nature of his disability (e.g., a student with attention deficit hyperactivity disorder being challenged to attend to instruction because where he is seated exacerbates his tendency to be inattentive). Accommodations are intended to provide the student with the highest probability possible to be able to learn from instruction—provided it is of high quality and the student puts forth the effort that is required.

A modification is a change in the core curriculum standard such that the student will learn different content. An example is a situation that involves each student in a classroom being taught math but, when this occurs, one student will work to learn basic addition facts while all of the others will learn the core curriculum standard that focuses on double digit addition with regrouping. The first student's targeted learning outcome will still be tied to the core curriculum, but it will be tied to a different, lower level standard. Thus, it is a modification.

Testing Accommodations

The collection of certain assessment data will involve accommodations that are provided on behalf of certain students with disabilities. Accommodations involve a change to the conditions under which an assessment is conducted and are intended to result in a more valid indication of a student's performance than would otherwise be the case without their use.

For example, if a student's specific learning disability impairs his ability to read, his performance on a math test that required him to read word problems might not be a valid representation of his math skills (both math calculation and reasoning) and more a representation of his limited reading skills. Similarly, the performance of a student with a physical disability that impairs his fine motor skills and ability to produce legible text on an English composition exam might not be a valid measure of his ability to actually compose an essay.

Time, Input, Student Response, and Setting

As was noted above, accommodations involve one or more of four areas: the time that a student is given to complete a task, the manner in which the task is presented to the student, the mode of responding that is required from the student, and the arrangement of the setting in which the task is to be performed. The accommodations that are provided should be predicated on a

specific student's needs rather than the fact that the student has been identified as having a particular disability (e.g., providing all students with a
specific learning disability an accommodation of being tested in a small
group arrangement). Below, examples of allowable accommodations are presented.

Time. Accommodations that apply to the amount of time that a student
has to complete a test include providing the student with extended
time (i.e., 1.5 times as long as allowed for others), permitting him to
take the test over multiple days, and embedding breaks during the time
allotted for the test.

Input. Accommodations that apply to how test items are presented to a
student include reading the directions, test items, and passages to him.

Response. Accommodations that apply to how the student will make responses to test items include allowing the student to type his responses
rather than write them by hand and dictating responses to a scribe.

Setting. Accommodations that apply to the features of the location in
which a student completes a test could include placement in a small
group or preferential seating such as at the front of the room and
facing the instructor.

RESPONSE-TO-INTERVENTION ASSESSMENT AND THE ROLE OF THE TEACHER

Focusing on Teaching Before Assessment

The role that a teacher fills as a member of an educational team is that of an
instructional expert.[6] Consequently, teachers need to be knowledgeable
about assessment and skilled at conducting certain types of assessment.
However, overall, it is fair to say that the primary concern of most teachers
about how assessment applies to their work is how it informs their instruction.

This situation calls to mind the evolution of the use of personal computers
by teachers in the classroom. Initially teachers were taught how to write
computer programs that they would then use to teach their students. Not too
long afterward, the focus shifted to training teachers how to use productivity
software (e.g., word processing and spreadsheet programs) to complete administrative tasks and educational software to present lessons, while others
wrote the programs for these activities.

Similarly, unlike a board-licensed clinical psychologist who is highly
knowledgeable about many assessments and is skilled in their administration,
the teacher's role in terms of assessments is to know a bit about certain
assessments and possess the skills to administer them. A teacher also needs

to be very knowledgeable about how to use the information obtained from an assessment to drive instruction.

Given this circumstance, there are three reasons why a chapter on assessment was not placed at the beginning of the book. One is that until the time when the screener is administered, its results analyzed, and students subsequently are placed in one of the framework's intervention tiers, teachers will be presenting instruction. Chances are that they will be doing so within a framework that does, in some manner, mimic a response-to-intervention framework (e.g., many schools have multidisciplinary teams that work with general education teachers to develop interventions for students who are not demonstrating expected outcomes).

A second reason is because teachers will not want to wait until all of the screening activities are completed before beginning to present effective, high quality instruction. The third reason is that teachers are more focused on learning how to present more effective instruction because this matter occupies more of their job description than does assessment. A time study analysis would confirm this assertion—in spite of concerns about the total amount of time that assessments are being conducted by teachers. Effective teachers use assessment to inform instruction, and this depiction of assessment emphasizes that teaching trumps assessment from a teacher's perspective.

The effective teaching literature has established the fact that effective teachers use data to drive their instructional decisions.[7] Accordingly, data-based decision making is a key element of a framework. What is less clear is the extent to which teachers need to be knowledgeable about the various types of assessments that are called for in a response-to-intervention framework, as well as skilled at conducting these assessments.[8]

Hence, one premise of this book is that beginning teachers, or teachers new to a response-to-intervention framework, need to be knowledgeable about the assessment component that is involved. Subsequently they will work with their building administrators to develop the amount and type of assessment expertise they will need to be effective in their job.

Testing or Teaching

A primary reason why a teacher wants to teach students how to take a test is so that everyone can be reasonably certain that the results are a valid representation of the student's knowledge of the subject matter that is tested. For instance, a student who does not understand how to select his answer may have known the correct answer but could not demonstrate this knowledge on a high stakes test because he did not know how to submit his response.

This circumstance highlights at least two issues for teachers: being able to make a basic distinction between teaching and testing plus dedicating an appropriate amount of time to teaching students how to take a test.

Making a basic distinction between teaching and testing can be explained through the work of a consultant who commented about the frustration he felt when he routinely observed what he regarded to be a testing protocol that teachers regarded to be an instructional strategy. One example was a teacher who was attempting to teach a vocabulary lesson that involved learning the names of animals.

The teacher would show the student a picture of an animal and then ask him, "What is the name of this animal?" Quite often a student would not respond because he did not know the name. Given the student's circumstances (age, presence of a disability) the student probably had not been taught the name and, therefore, could not respond to the teacher's directive which amounted to a test rather than what the teacher thought was a teaching procedure.

As was discussed previously, testing is the means by which the presence of something is determined. In schools, tests determine the presence of a student's knowledge, possession of a skill, or the ability to perform a task. Mostly a test consists of the presentation of a stimulus, or some type of directive, to which a student must provide a response independently. Examples include a teacher presenting the directive, "Spell the word 'dog,'" the written instruction, "List three reasons that have been identified as a cause for the Civil War" on a history test, or "Graph the linear equation $3x + 7$" on an algebra test.

Teaching, on the other hand, involves some type of teacher action after presenting or referring to a task directive. Specifically, teaching entails one of four basic teacher actions: presenting written instructions, oral instructions, modeling, or physical prompts.

CHAPTER 6 COMPREHENSION CHECK

Now that you have finished reading the chapter, you should be able to:

- List the elements of an RTI framework's assessment component.
- Identify the differences between assessment, evaluation, and testing.
- Explain how assessment can either inform instruction or act as a barrier.
- Explain what is meant by a "high-stakes test."
- List the issues schools must address when they administer a high stakes test.
- Discuss how the items that comprise an RTI framework's assessment component are but one part of a school's assessment milieu.
- Distinguish between informal and formal assessment, formative and summative assessment, and criterion and norm-referenced assessment.
- Describe testing accommodations and list two examples.

NOTES

1. National Center on Response-to-intervention, "RTI Implementer Series: Module 1: Screening—Training Manual," (Washington, DC: U.S. Department of Education, Office of Special Education Programs, National Center on Response-to-intervention, 2012).

2. National Center on Response-to-intervention, "RTI Implementer Series: Module 2: Progress Monitoring—Training Manual," (Washington, DC: U.S. Department of Education, Office of Special Education Programs, National Center on Response-to-intervention, 2012).

3. Daryl F. Mellard and Evelyn Johnson, *RTI: A Practitioner's Guide to Implementing Response-to-intervention* (Thousand Oaks, CA: Corwin Press. 2008).

4. Douglas Fuchs and Lynn S. Fuchs, "Introduction to Response-to-intervention: What, Why, and How Valid is It?" *Reading Research Quarterly* 41, no. 1 (2006): 93–99.

5. Pamela Stecker, Douglas Fuchs, and Lynn S. Fuchs, "Progress Monitoring as Essential Practice Within Response-to-intervention," *Rural Special Education Quarterly* 27, no. 4 (2008): 10–17.

6. Mark Wolery, Melinda Jones Ault, and Patricia Munson Doyle, *Teaching Students with Moderate to Severe Disabilities: Use of Response Prompting Strategies,* ed. by Naomi Silverman (White Plains, NY: Longman Publishing Group, 1992).

7. Jere Brophy, "Teacher Influences on Student Achievement," *American Psychologist* 41, no. 10 (1986): 1069–1077, http://dx.doi.org/10.1037/0003-066X.41.10.1069.

8. Ibid.

Chapter Seven

Practical Considerations

OVERVIEW

In this chapter you will learn about a number of practical considerations that are involved in the design and operation of a response-to-intervention framework. Key points from the chapter include the following:

Each school that designs and implements an RTI framework must address numerous practical matters that involve the school's unique circumstances as well as the framework's design.

To implement the RTI framework's assessment component schools will need to identify the instruments that will be administered, the personnel who will administer them and how the data will be interpreted for the purpose of identifying which students will receive services in each of the RTI framework's intervention tiers.

Proper school-wide supervision will involve ensuring the fidelity of implementation of the RTI framework as well as its coordination across classrooms in the same grade (horizontal coordination) and classrooms across grade levels or schools (vertical coordination).

Professional development activities will need to address the design and implementation of a school's specific RTI framework. Other professional development topics may include the explicit meaning of high-quality instruction and how to administer a particular screener or progress monitoring assessment.

Fidelity of implementation issues include monitoring the presentation of high-quality instruction in Tier 1, intensive intervention in small group arrangements in Tier 2, and appropriate special education services in Tier 3. The services across tiers must not simply be "more of the same," yet they need to account for the services provided in other tiers.

Schools will need to be cognizant of transparent and hidden expenditures that are involved with the implementation of a response-to-intervention framework. Transparent costs are those that are readily identifiable, such as the cost of instructional materials and assessment instruments. Hidden costs are not as readily identifiable and could include the value of a staff member's time spent supervising the work of volunteers, or school staff foregoing other beneficial activities such as attending a professional conference.

Implementation of a response-to-intervention framework in middle and high schools will involve protocols that are specific to the way these schools' function. For instance, students' grades in previous years' courses may supplant the use of a universal screener and Tier 2 services may be provided through a course (e.g., a lab) rather than an end-of-the-day "What I Need" school-wide activity period.

PRACTICAL CONSIDERATIONS

From the outset of this book the framework has been described as a way to design a process for the purpose of determining how to provide services that not only would enable every student to master the content in the general education curriculum but also assist with the identification of students with disabilities who are eligible to receive special education services. As such, a response-to-intervention framework provides broad, general guidelines concerning how to proceed. This means that it sets the stage for many questions to be raised, thereby requiring the educators who use the framework to provide or generate satisfactory answers to these questions.

While the framework can be used at any level within a school system to direct the work that school personnel perform, its implementation at each school will result in somewhat unique sets of questions and answers. Also, the framework sets the occasion for more questions to be raised than it provides answers to these questions.

While it is beyond the scope of this book—or any other book for that matter—to address this topic in a way that would be appropriate for every school—what is appropriate to do is identify and discuss a number of practical considerations that, most likely, will be relevant for most building level educators, meaning administrators and staff. What is sometimes said about the actual implementation of any broad framework that is easy to describe and appears to be very appropriate applies to the discussion, that follows, about the RTI framework: the devil lies in the details.

While this topic was broached in chapter 1 and referenced at various times throughout chapters 2–6, the information presented below is a more detailed discussion compared to what has been presented previously. This information was not addressed in detail in the preceding chapters because the intent of these chapters was to enable you to clearly focus on the teacher's role in the framework. In this chapter a much more detailed discussion of the numerous and varied issues that must be addressed across a number of a school's stakeholders is presented.

Implementation of the framework is a labor-intensive endeavor, and a framework's effectiveness will depend, in large measure, on the degree to which these issues are addressed satisfactorily. In many instances these issues will never be addressed definitively. Rather, they will need to be addressed routinely as circumstances warrant. Your consideration of this information will enable you to develop a deeper understanding of your role in the execution of your school's response-to-intervention framework, which may be thought of as its master intervention plan.

SCHOOL-WIDE WORK SCOPE

A school's first order of business when it sets out to implement a response-to-intervention framework is to identify what work needs to be performed.[1,2] In turn, this work scope will lead to the identification of many related issues that need to be addressed. Put another way, to effectively and efficiently implement a framework one needs to know the relevant questions that need to be asked and answered.

Your awareness of this circumstance should result in you developing a greater appreciation for how the resource intensive nature of the framework affects administrators and teachers alike. An example of a school-wide work scope that would be appropriate for the three tier response-to-intervention framework that has been discussed in this book includes the following:

Assessment

1. Integration of the RTI framework's assessment component with all of the school's other assessment activities
2. Selection of screening instruments with sound psychometric properties
3. Schedule for the administration of the screening instruments
4. Analysis of the data obtained from the administration of the screening instruments, to include decisions about students' placements in the intervention tiers
5. Selection of the student progress monitoring instruments with sound psychometric properties
6. Schedule for the administration of the student progress monitoring assessments

7. Analysis of the data obtained from the administration of the student progress monitoring assessments to include the consideration of all other available assessment data and subsequent decisions about students' placements in the intervention tiers

8. Protocol for multidisciplinary evaluation and eligibility determinations for special education services

Intervention Services

1. Presentation of high-quality instruction in each general education classroom

2. Presentation of intensive, effective, small group Tier 2 intervention services

3. Provision of appropriate Tier 3 special education services

Supervision

1. Schoolwide coordination of the implementation of a framework

2. Schoolwide supervision of the fidelity of implementation of the framework

SCHOOL-SPECIFIC ISSUES

A school will have to decide which personnel will implement its response-to-intervention framework. These personnel may include both paid staff and volunteers. It will be easy to identify some personnel, such as the general education teachers who will be tasked to provide high quality Tier 1 instruction in the general education classroom as well as the special education teachers who will be tasked to provide many of the Tier 3 intervention services. The identification of the other personnel who will be involved and the work they perform will be more challenging.

Assessment Personnel

The instruments that are used to conduct the assessments that are called for in a response-to-intervention framework will stipulate who is qualified to administer them. Most likely, general and special education teachers will administer most of the screening and progress monitoring assessments. However, other personnel such as school psychologists, licensed psychologists, and psychometrists will conduct many of the assessments that are involved in an evaluation for determining a student's eligibility for the receipt of special education services. Additionally, these assessments will be conducted in accordance with applicable federal, state and local laws and regulations.

Tier 2 Personnel

The identification, or designation, of the personnel who will provide Tier 2 intervention services highlights how each school will have a unique RTI framework and how its implementation will depend upon available resources. In some schools the general education teacher will be tasked to provide both Tier 1 and Tier 2 intervention services in her classroom. In other schools a special education teacher may be tasked to provide Tier 2 small group intervention services alongside a general education teacher in her classroom or separately in another location within the school.

Other schools may employ reading specialists, instructional assistants, school psychologists, behavior specialists or generic intervention specialists (e.g., a person who provides Tier 2 intervention services across more than one academic discipline using commercial programs) to provide Tier 2 intervention services. Another option is to solicit the help of non-paid personnel, such as volunteers from the community (e.g., parents, grandparents, retirees), college students who must complete a practicum experience or college and high school students who must perform community service work. Using volunteers involves other issues that are not addressed below.

Implementation Fidelity

A school administrator or her designee will have to perform work to ensure the fidelity of implementation of all aspects of the framework. This will involve validating that each component is both implemented when it is scheduled and how it is to be implemented (e.g., standardized screeners and progress monitoring assessments, high quality instruction in general education classrooms).

School-Wide Coordination

School-wide coordination involves, but certainly is not limited to, addressing the matters below.

Horizontal and Vertical Alignment

Horizontal alignment refers to coordination across classrooms at the same grade level. This alignment could be managed by a school administrator, or her designee, which might be one of the grade level teachers who is designated to be the lead teacher for her grade. Vertical alignment refers to coordination across grade levels, as well as schools (e.g., student transitions from elementary to middle school). It, too, could be managed by a school leader, or her designees, which could be the aforementioned lead teacher. Additionally, a district level team could be created to oversee this work.

General and Special Education

The way that general and special education teachers' interface will have to be addressed while accounting for both the services that are called for in students' IEPs and the school's RTI framework. Whereas general-education teachers' primary task will be to present high-quality instruction in the general education classroom, special education teachers may be called upon to perform a wide variety of tasks that could include co-teaching in general education classrooms, providing accommodations and modifications for students with disabilities in these classrooms, and providing Tier 2 and Tier 3 intervention services.

An important issue that will have to be resolved with respect to the role of special education teachers is the extent to which they are direct services providers or the extent to which they present instruction, as opposed to functioning as a case manager. Direct service provision could include rotating with the general education teacher to present both large and small group instruction and re-teaching a lesson to a small group of students after the teacher has presented the core lesson.

Indirect service provision and case management tasks may include assisting students with organizational skills, redirecting students' attention during a lesson, making modified instructional materials, recording behavior data, and implementing accommodations and modifications. Some have depicted the special education teacher's performance in this regard as one of "value added."

Coordination with other professionals who provide special education services also will need to be addressed. These professionals include, but certainly are not limited to, speech-language pathologists, occupational and physical therapists, and school psychologists. These professionals will interface with both general and special education teachers as well as both students with mild and moderate or more significant disabilities.

Professional Development

Professional development will be both wide ranging and ongoing.[3,4,5,6] Furthermore, while the topics that are addressed might be dictated by a school district, the most relevant and timely professional development will be that which is settled upon by a school.

An initial training will have to address the school's response-to-intervention framework: its design (e.g., the assessment component as well as the number of intervention tiers and the purpose of each tier) and every staff member's role in the framework. This training highlights why a school will be best served when it controls its professional development activities.

High-Quality Instruction

A school will have to operationally define high quality instruction and then determine the topics that will be addressed in trainings concerning it. Factors such as the typical turnover rate of a school's staff and the differences in their teacher preparation programs will be prime considerations when identifying topics.

Schools that typically experience high rates of staff attrition may have to routinely provide training on fundamental topics such as their school's response-to-intervention framework, how to administer the instruments in the assessment protocol, universal effective teaching practices, evidence-based interventions in each of the academic disciplines, intensive small group and 1:1 instruction, special education services, and the school's programming that pertains to teaching students appropriate school social behaviors. Schools that typically experience low rates of staff attrition may initially address their professional development needs through their hiring process.

That is to say, through this process they might seek to hire someone with relatively limited professional development needs. Applicant interviews may be designed and conducted to determine a candidate's knowledge about—as well as knowledge and preservice training with respect to—administering assessments, providing effective instruction using evidence-based practices, and providing intensive small group and 1:1 instruction. After an applicant is hired, she may receive most of her training from similarly situated colleagues who have been employed at the school for a number of years rather than from whole school staff professional development sessions.

Assessment

Given the plethora of available assessment instruments and the variance that exists across teacher certification programs, it is highly unlikely that most teachers will be ready to administer the instruments that have been selected to implement a response-to-intervention framework's assessment component. Schools, therefore, will have to provide relevant professional development.

Specifically, they will need to adhere to the training requirements that are stipulated by the publisher regarding the administration of the assessment. Additionally, professional development will need to address how to analyze the data that are obtained from the administration of an assessment for the purpose of how each student will be placed in one of the framework's tiers. When possible, the data need to be analyzed with respect to how they can inform the presentation of instruction.

Whenever high stakes testing is related to the framework, aspects of this testing will have to be addressed in detail during professional development activities. Teachers will need to know what they need to do to meet the requirements that pertain to high stakes testing (e.g., the curriculum they need to teach) as well as what they need to tell their students about this testing and how to document that they told the students this information.

Teacher Preparation Programs

Perhaps the "500-pound gorilla in the room" with respect to any response-to-intervention framework is the role that teacher preparation programs play. The topic of professional development highlights the ill-defined, yet important, role that teacher preparation programs play with regard to response-to-intervention frameworks. Irrespective of how a teacher was educated prior to being employed, at a minimum they need to be provided professional development that addresses their school's particular response-to-intervention framework.

Curriculum and Instructional Materials

As you know by now, central to the framework is the provision of high-quality instruction in the general education classroom. In chapter 2, high-quality instruction was operationally defined along five dimensions, with one being a focus on the core curriculum. Hence, consideration of a school's core curriculum and the instructional materials that will be used to teach it in the general education classroom is central to a school's effective implementation of its framework.

As a practical matter, educators will need to clearly define the curriculum so that everyone who provides instruction will be in agreement on the knowledge and skills that will be taught. Presently some of the state standards are written in a way that prevents even two educators from readily agreeing to what the standards actually mean.

Additionally, many schools go through a formal process to decide upon the commercial program that will be purchased to support the teaching of the curriculum. This process needs to be conducted with the concept of high-quality instruction in mind. Teachers will need to be provided training about how to use the program, and then fidelity checks will need to be conducted to ensure the correct and consistent implementation of the program across classrooms.

When commercial materials are adopted for use in the general education classroom, one related question that must be answered is what materials will be adopted for use in Tier 2 and Tier 3. Considering the characteristics of Tier 2 and Tier 3 services (e.g., focus on teaching fewer skills), these materials should provide for the repetition students need while maintaining their interest. Furthermore, from the outset what needs to be explained are the ways in which the services that are provided in Tiers 2 and Tier 3 will be markedly different from the services in Tier 1.

TIER CONSIDERATIONS

Lateral movement within a tier (e.g., within Tier 1, first moving a student to a different general education classroom instead of placing the student in Tier 2).

This consideration highlights the need to develop a way to ensure consistency across classrooms. After defining high-quality instruction educators will need to ensure some type of consistency regarding the provision of high-quality instruction across classrooms. Inconsistency in any aspect of the delivery of high-quality instruction means that educators will have to answer at least two questions: (a) what steps will be taken to assist a teacher in presenting high quality instruction in her classroom and (b) which procedures will be followed if it is believed that moving a student to another classroom in his grade level—a move that could be labeled as a lateral move within Tier 1— would be an appropriate intervention?

Location of Intervention Services

Tier 1 instruction will be presented in general education classrooms with large group arrangements (twenty to thirty or more students with one teacher). However, RTI frameworks call for small group instruction in Tier 2 and Tier 3. Thus, a practical matter that will need to be addressed is the location where Tier 2 and Tier 3 intervention services will be provided. Three options include the general education classroom, a room that is designed for small group instruction, or a dual-purpose location (e.g., the general education classroom, the cafeteria during non-use to avoid possible distractions, a conference room, a room in separate building or on the stage in a gymnasium).

Some of the issues that will have to be addressed when Tier 2 intervention services are provided in a general education classroom include the following:

1. Designating who will provide the services
2. Proper supervision of all of the students who are not in the group if the general education teacher presents Tier 2 intervention services
3. Constructing a location that is conducive to presenting small group instruction
4. Minimizing disruptions and distractions to both the students who are and are not members of the group

5. Considering how students who receive Tier 2 or Tier 3 services might be negatively stigmatized

When these services are provided outside of the general education classroom this arrangement allows for everyone to consider how the core, or general education curriculum, can be taught beyond the general education setting. This is a very important consideration because throughout a framework the focus is on providing instruction/interventions to students to enable them to master the general education curriculum.

For a number of reasons, including students who do not want their peers to be able to observe them receiving Tier 2 or Tier 3 services, locations within a school other than the general education classroom may be where Tier 2 and Tier 3 services are provided in small group arrangements. As was noted in chapters 4 and 5, features of these locations mirror those of a general education classroom (e.g., lines of sight, aesthetics, limiting distractions). This might mean that furniture and other items will need to be purchased for these locations.

Criteria for Moving Students Across Tiers and Length of Time in Tiers

A school will have to set criteria for moving students across tiers, to include referring a student for an evaluation for a determination of eligibility for special education services

It is relatively easy to establish criteria for the minimum length of time a student must remain in a tier. For instance, one common practice is to have a student receive Tier 2 intervention services for a period of time that is equal to one grading period (e.g., six or nine weeks). A challenge that often arises is what to do with students who make progress in Tier 2 but not in a way that allows for a return to Tier 1, nor in a way that indicates that a referral for a special education eligibility determination is warranted. One way to address this challenge is to provide these students with ultra-intensive Tier 2 instruction.

How to Use the Framework When Norm-Referenced/Locally Established Benchmarks/Proficiency Standards are Not Met

A very practical matter that educators will have to address is establishing the benchmarks and proficiency standards that will be used for identifying the students who are making adequate progress in the core curriculum, and therefore, will continue to receive the Tier 1 services, as well as the students who have not met the benchmarks and, as a result, need to receive additional services in either Tier 2 or Tier 3.[7] If this matter is not addressed properly the number of Tier 2 and Tier 3 students might approach the number of Tier 1 students.

In some instances, norm-referenced benchmarks have been established and will be appropriate to use. For example, benchmarks for critical, fundamental reading skills (e.g., naming the upper- and lowercase letters of the alphabet and decoding non-words) that are strongly correlated to becoming a proficient reader by the end of the third grade have been established. Likewise, criterion-referenced, grade level standards for certain skills have been established.

In an ideal world, these benchmarks would be used to identify no more than the 20–25 percent of students that a response-to-intervention framework estimates will need to receive Tier 2 services. Yet, the reality is that less than 20 percent of the students in some schools will fail to meet these benchmarks whereas in other schools well more than 25 percent of the students will fail to meet the benchmarks.

Schools in which fewer than 20 percent of the students fail to meet the benchmarks can use a response-to-intervention framework as it has been described in this book, in terms of the focus of Tier 2 (at-risk students) and Tier 3 services. On the other hand, educators in schools in which more than 25 percent of the students fail to meet benchmarks will have to consider how the framework can be configured so that its basic structure remains intact as the needs of all students are addressed.

At first glance, the latter circumstance described above would appear to render the use of an RTI framework as totally impractical. That is to say, if more than 25 percent of the students fail to meet benchmarks one might quickly conclude that there are not enough resources available to provide each of the students who need to receive them either Tier 2 or Tier 3 services. Rather than this being the case, the framework needs to be maintained and the services that are provided in each tier reconfigured. For instance,

1. In Tier 1 critique how high-quality instruction is being presented, paying particular attention to whether there is a need to increase the amount of allocated time (e.g., reduce or eliminate non-essential activities, such as unsupervised learning centers, peer groups that do not adhere to the use of accountable talk and frequent demonstrations of on-task behavior), follow a more streamlined curriculum scope and sequence or present more small group instruction to at-risk students.
2. Still provide Tier 2 services but increase the size of each group and reduce the number of days per week and time per session.
3. Tier 3 services must be considered with an understanding of the two-part special education eligibility criteria. This criterion highlights the fact that a student who is determined to be eligible to receive special education services must be functioning in such a way, because of the

disability, so as to need specially-designed instruction. In situations in which there is a relatively large number of students who are not meeting proficiency standards, it can be extremely difficult to identify no-disabled students who are low performers from students that meet the criteria for a disability.

This circumstance highlights how the framework results in the provision of individualized instruction in a manner that is similar to the special education mandate that this type of instruction be provided to students with disabilities. While the framework can be used to identify students with disabilities, inherent in its use with all students is a focus on establishing individualized instructional conditions under which each student's data indicates that he is making meaningful progress in the general education curriculum.

Establishing Site-Specific Benchmarks for Appropriate School Social Behavior

The display of certain behaviors, particularly appropriate school social behaviors that are dependent upon the context in which they are displayed, will have to be evaluated based upon local benchmarks. Whereas guidelines are available for the age at which students should perform certain adaptive behaviors (such as toileting oneself independently or using a spoon, fork, and knife to eat), these guidelines are not available for social behaviors that students are expected to display so as to be in compliance with the expectations that have been established for a school.

In these instances, mechanisms, such as the publication of a student handbook, should be created to teach students what to do rather than what not to do (e.g., Wear shirts with a collar and pants made of whole cloth). Likewise, a core school social behavior curriculum that is aligned with staff expectations and is taught to students needs to be adopted. Upon completion of these tasks, benchmarks can be established for the purpose of identifying students in need of Tier 2 and Tier 3 services.

Tier 2 services could be defined as services that have been designed for students who engage in disruptive behaviors that impede not only theirs but also other students' mastery of academic skills and school social behaviors. Furthermore, students who need Tier 2 intervention services present challenges in establishing healthy relationships with others. Hence, Tier 2 interventions would attempt to teach students to conform with existing school guidelines.

Tier 3 services would be provided to students whose school social behaviors present a danger to self or others. Danger would be broadly defined to include self-injurious behaviors, physical or verbal assault, and property damage. Tier 3 interventions would be highly-focused in an attempt to keep students out of more restrictive placements (e.g., juvenile justice, day treatment facility, therapeutic day treatment program).

Prospect of Providing Purposeful Instruction to all Students

The good news is that, if implemented with fidelity, a response-to-intervention framework results in all students receiving purposeful, individualized instruction. However, with the option of moving a student onto another tier and moving the primary responsibility for the student's instruction on to another teacher, there may be a temptation to not try too hard to investigate what else can be done to enable the student to be successful in his current tier.

This phenomenon may also occur in a special education eligibility determination model in which an ability-achievement formula is used to identify students who have a specific learning disability. In this model, a teacher might conclude that a student would be better served if the teacher withheld remedial instruction so that his academic achievement scores would drop to a level that is discrepant enough with his ability scores in order to meet the special education eligibility criteria as a child with a specific learning disability.

On the one hand, educators do not want to leave a student in a tier beyond the point in time when it becomes readily apparent that there is reason to believe that he may benefit from the differential services that will be provided in another tier. On the other hand, educators do not want to move a student to another tier when adjustments to the current tier can be made in the belief that he can make adequate progress by using these adjustments.

If educators are not careful, they might populate a tier outside of the general education classroom such that the services that are to be provided in these tiers are so watered down as to make the distinguishing features of the tier unrecognizable. For example, creating a Tier 2 small group arrangement in which eight to eleven students are to receive meaningful instruction to assist them in their general education English, math, and social studies classes essentially results in a miniature Tier 1 classroom. If this were to happen it may result from a good faith effort to match each student to the most appropriate, albeit extremely limited, resources available.

Foregoing Tiers When the Need to do so is Evident

Some students, such as those with significant intellectual disabilities, will need to be provided special education services at the earliest moment possible. This might mean that a student does not spend time in Tier 1 and bypasses Tier 2 entirely.[8] The IDEA's least restrictive environment requirement and continuum of alternative placements allow for this situation. However, you must remain mindful that the program for every student with disability must account for how he can be involved in instructional programs and extracurricular activities with nondisabled peers to the maximum extent appropriate.

Continuing Tier 1 Services while Providing Tier 2 and 3 Intervention Services

The schedule that will be created and followed so that students continue to receive instruction in their general education classrooms while also receiving Tier 2 and Tier 3 intervention services will present a challenge. Scheduling across classrooms can be a trying experience, especially in an elementary school where every general education teacher presents her literacy instruction during the same instructional time block each day. This circumstance highlights the fact that a school's administration will have to be intimately involved in the design and implementation of its response-to-intervention framework.

Perception of Tier 2 and Tier 3 Intervention Services

School personnel need to consider discussing among stakeholders—meaning staff, parents, and students—how a student's success outside of Tier 1 will be viewed. Central to this view will have to be the non-judgmental perspective that differential Tier 2 and Tier 3 services are appropriate and do not necessarily imply that they are inherently better than the services that are being presented in a general education classroom. In other words, if a student demonstrates mastery of the general education curriculum after receiving Tier 2 services this does not mean the Tier 1 instruction was inadequate because of the teacher who provided it. Quite the contrary—particularly when high quality instruction has been operationally defined and verified.

Rather, Tier 2 intervention services might result in the conditions the student needed to be placed under to be able to be successful. This approach also allows for a discussion regarding how Tier 2 services may need to be presented in the future as opposed to being a treatment that has "cured," or resolved, a student's learning challenges. These services may enable students who do not meet the eligibility criteria for special education services but are habitually considered to be low achievers to achieve expected learning outcomes throughout their school careers.

Assessment

The assessments that will be conducted in each tier involve certain features that warrant consideration. Tier 2 and Tier 3 are characterized, in part, by the administration of more frequent assessments (i.e., formative), and these assessments will be tied to fewer skills. Additional issues that will need to be considered include the assessments' alignments with the general education curriculum as well as their technical adequacy (e.g., validity and reliability).

Time for Assessments and Assessment-Related Activities

The schedule and process that will be followed to record and periodically review assessment data, and the criteria and process for making a referral for a special education eligibility evaluation, need to be established. Questions that will need to be asked and answered include:

1. Will the data be centrally located on a website or maintained offline in files?
2. Will a multidisciplinary team review the data?
3. Who will be a member of the team?
4. Will post-meeting reports be written, and who will be provided with copies of the report?
5. Will "Actionable" recommendations be provided to interventionists, and follow-up observations be conducted for the purpose of ensuring the recommendations were implemented and the results from them are valid?
6. How will caregivers be informed about the assessment data?

EXPENDITURES

While a preservice or beginning teacher will mostly be concerned with classroom-level considerations that readily affect their provision of direct services to students, others will be concerned about more all-encompassing considerations, including the costs that pertain to an RTI framework. Ultimately, however, the cost of the framework will directly impact every teacher and student. Consequently, the costs that are involved in the design and implementation of the framework are, to varying degrees, a practical consideration for everyone involved.

Undoubtedly these costs will be a major determinant in the design, implementation and effectiveness of the specific framework a school adopts. For relevant cost considerations to be valid they will have to be evaluated within the context of the purpose of the framework. This purpose, which was discussed in chapter 1 when the history of the framework was addressed, is reviewed before an overview of cost considerations is presented.

Purpose of the RTI framework

The purpose of the framework is to provide school personnel with a systematic protocol that enables them to individualize instruction by matching students with the services that address their needs. Hence, it can be viewed as a proactive approach since it calls for ongoing assessment and the use of the data obtained to keep students in instructional programs that are designed to meet their unique needs and result in their attainment of targeted learning outcomes. These outcomes are intended to be the students' mastery of age- and grade-level core curriculum content.

Thus, as a result of its design and implementation the framework provides school personnel with mechanisms for presenting effective instruction to every student. Schools are equipped with a plan for success as opposed to being incentivized to allow students to demonstrate low achievement so that they can be provided additional, individualized services. Specifically, these would be special education services.

Nonetheless, some have characterized the RTI framework, with its emphasis on the provision of high-quality, evidence-based instruction in general education classrooms, as a preventative approach. They see the framework as a protocol that prevents two types of failure. One type is the failure of any student to attain age- and grade-level targeted learning outcomes. A second type is the failure of school personnel to accurately identify students with disabilities who are eligible to receive relatively costly special education services—particularly students with a specific learning disability who comprise nearly 50 percent of all students who have been determined to be eligible to receive these services.

In fact, before the framework was introduced school personnel often decried what they referred to as the "wait to fail" approach that had been used to identify students with a specific learning disability. This meant that, in order to receive additional services, students had to demonstrate a failure to achieve that was significantly discrepant from their measured potential to learn. Many believed that this circumstance created a disincentive to teach certain students.

The inaccurate identification of students with disabilities highlights several concerns, some of which were addressed in chapter 1. One concern that is relevant to the present discussion is the over identification of students as having disabilities, a phenomenon that has been referred to as false positives. In this context a false positive refers to a student who meets the eligibility criteria for the receipt of special education services, but the reason for this eligibility is not an inherent, biologically based disability. Rather, the reason the student demonstrates low academic achievement just like some of his classmates who do not have a disability is because the aforementioned student has received inappropriately designed instruction.

Further, there is reason to believe that this instruction could be effective because evidence-based knowledge about effective instruction is available, as are supporting resources, such as the instructional materials that are used when a standard treatment protocol is followed to provide Tier 2 services. These circumstances partly, but significantly, contributed to the initial development of the RTI framework.

This discussion highlights why cost considerations are an important element of an RTI framework. While special education is, relatively speaking, a costly undertaking that is to be avoided—especially when it is unwarranted and, therefore, unnecessary—the design and implementation of an RTI framework is also a costly undertaking. However, it is reasonable to conclude that any such mechanism to account for the performance outcome of every student will involve considerable costs.

Perhaps what is at issue in the minds of some are not only the expenditures associated with the framework but also whether there is a noteworthy cost savings from it use as is implied by those who make the over identification argument presented above. In other words, in a school with five hundred students are only two or twenty-two of them going to avoid being improperly identified as needing special education services?

This introduction sets the stage for an examination of the costs directly involved in, or associated with, the design and implementation of an RTI framework by a school or larger parent organization, such as a school district. In the discussion below both sides of the ledger, meaning available funds and expenses, that potentially are associated with the framework are identified and discussed. The term "potentially" is meaningful because chances are that schools will not pinpoint the exact cost of the framework given the detailed work involved. One reason this is the case is because in many instances separating an RTI expense from a "business as usual" expense will be very imprecise.

For instance, schools routinely present large group instruction in a general education classroom. If a school were to adopt an RTI framework and, because they did so, conducted a detailed search process for the purpose of selecting new instructional and assessment materials that were evidence-based, this could be considered an RTI framework expense. Conversely, if they instituted the framework but simply decided to go with some of the resources they already have plus of few additional new materials, then this type of expense would be difficulty to calculate precisely.

A second reason why pinpointing the exact cost of the framework most likely will be imprecise is because schools do not account for employee salaries in the same way as other professions. For instance, accountants and attorneys who charge for billable hours that are documented in fifty-minute increments can readily identify salary expenses in terms of the exact work that was performed.

While schools can determine their employees' hourly rates, in the course of a workday, schools typically do not have employees complete timesheets on which they document their specific activities. Consequently, when an employee attends a meeting to review the assessment data for a student who is receiving Tier 2 services the time the employee spends in this meeting is not tracked, specifically, as an RTI cost. Hence, the discussion in this section makes one aware of potential RTI costs that school personnel can consider how to track and plan for.

Since the determination of the overall cost of an RTI framework most likely will be imprecise, from the outset those concerned with cost considerations may want to simultaneously consider answers to other related and relevant key questions since these answers may justify using the framework in spite of the cost for doing so. These questions include (a) whether the framework is a well-reasoned approach to addressing school accountability; (b) is the framework based on some sense of practical utility, meaning is it more than a theoretical construct); (c) does any research exist to support its effectiveness; and, (d) does its use allow for some way to track its costs so that this information can be used to make decisions about the framework's continued use?

Available funds

While references to cost considerations implies the need to exclusively examine expenditures, it is important to appraise both sides of the ledger if there is reason to do so. As for the RTI framework, there are existing sources of revenue for implementing it. Furthermore, use of the framework might result in cost savings that can be re-appropriated as funding for the framework.

One revenue source is the IDEA. When Congress reauthorized the IDEA in 2004, the Congress stated that school districts could use 15 percent of IDEA's Part B funds to provide early intervening services and could combine these funds with other available federal funds (e.g. from the Elementary and Secondary Education Act)[9] An RTI framework is one example of an early intervening service, which is a service that is designed to address a student's lack of attainment of targeted learning outcomes at the earliest possible moment for the purpose of not only remediating the learning challenge but also enabling the student to continuously make adequate progress in his age- and grade-level core curriculum.

Additionally, the IDEA could, at any point in time, be a source of additional revenue in another way. This could occur if the Congress lived up to its original pledge to fund 40 percent of a state's costs of providing special education services. Congress has never provided this level of funding, which would offset the framework's Tier 3 costs. Rather, the Congress has provided funding that has covered anywhere from 7 percent to 19 percent of these costs.[10] School personnel could contribute to a grass roots advocacy movement that most likely would be needed to generate this additional source of revenue.

A second revenue source for the framework is the money being spent for existing efforts that are being undertaken for somewhat similar purposes. An example is the prereferral-to-placement process that is followed by many schools. While this process is identified by many different names, it refers to the protocol schools follow to identify children with disabilities. It is one part of the IDEA's mandatory effort, called Child Find, to locate every child who needs to receive special education services.

A prereferral-to-placement process consists of multiple elements that include identifying children who are demonstrating low academic achievement and then providing remedial instruction to ameliorate the student's low performance. Other elements of the process include administering assessments and evaluating the data obtained, and performing administrative tasks (e.g., writing reports). Schools could discontinue this process because its work could be incorporated into the RTI framework. Consequently, the funds for the process could be re-appropriated to the RTI framework.

A third revenue source are the funds that will become available from a reduction in the provision of special education services. These funds can be considerable when calculated in terms of years of savings (i.e., the expenditures that would have resulted from the special education services a student was provided beginning in grade 3 through twelfth grade) rather than one-time eligibility determination savings.

Fourth, existing resources can be incorporated into the framework and be considered as a revenue source since they would eliminate the need to pay for them. These resources include existing before- and after-school tutoring programs, internet-based remedial instruction that is free to access once a person is able to use the internet, and learning strategies classes.

RTI expenses

When school personnel consider the potential RTI-related expenses that are identified and discussed below, they may benefit from thinking about them in terms of the type of expense that is involved. One way to think about the type of expense that is involved is in general terms with respect to whether the cost can be thought of as one that can be quantified or one that cannot. A second way to think about the type of expense that is involved is in more specific terms with respect to whether it is a transparent, hidden, or opportunity cost.

A transparent cost is one that is readily identifiable, meaning that an extraordinary effort does not need to be made to detect it. Most transparent costs can be readily identified through existing requisition protocols.

A hidden cost is a cost that exists but is relatively opaque. Thus, it can be determined through some type of extraordinary effort.

An example would be establishing a personnel expense protocol and then tracking the expenses that are based upon it. For instance, the hourly rates of school personnel who conduct clearly defined RTI activities, such as providing Tier 2 instruction or attending meetings where student assessment data are analyzed, could be determined and then used to calculate the cost of the RTI-related work they perform. To do this, these personnel would have to meticulously record the time they spent engaging in these activities.

Opportunity costs involve those that are associated with "what might have been, or could be," but for the need to address an RTI matter. Often these types of costs, for which several examples are provided below, cannot be quantified.

Next some of the potential costs that may be associated with the design and implementation of an RTI framework are identified and discussed.

1. Instructional and assessment materials. In some instances costs will be involved with the requisitioning of Tier 1 and Tier 2 instructional materials and assessment instruments. A key undertaking will be to establish a process that will result in the location of materials that are evidence-based and contribute to the provision of high-quality instruction.

    The costs associated with Tier 2 materials will depend upon whether a standard treatment or problem-solving protocol will be used. The standard treatment protocol involves the acquisition of commercial materials which also means that related costs may be incurred, including those for professional development and the storage of these materials. If a problem-solving protocol is used then existing materials may simply be repurposed to provide Tier 2 services.

    Regarding assessment instruments, their acquisition and use needs to be considered in the context of the school's assessment milieu. Two questions school personnel need to answer when considering whether to take on new expenditures related to assessment include (a) whether the new assessment activity results in the production of information that cannot be obtained elsewhere, such as through the administration of existing assessments, and (b) whether the new assessment activity informs instruction so that it becomes more effective or efficient.

2. Tier 2 facilities. There will be costs involved with the arrangement of the location where Tier 2 instruction will be presented. If this instruction is presented in general education classrooms then schools may

have to purchase items such as kidney-shaped tables, chairs, and portable dividers to allow for a proper environmental arrangement. Additionally, as was noted above, some type of storage capacity for instructional and assessment materials may have to be acquired. If this instruction is provided in another location, such as a portable building, then similar material costs as well as building maintenance and operation costs (e.g., utility costs) would be involved.

3. Labor costs for tiered or level instruction. The types of services that are provided in Tier 2 and Tier 3 of the framework highlight the labor-intensive aspect of educating students who demonstrate learning challenges. A school's per pupil expenditure increases significantly whenever the pupil:teacher ratio is lowered. Hence, this fact highlights the need to identify and fully develop the elements that comprise, and result in, high-quality, evidence-based, effective instruction in the large group arrangements that predominate in general education classrooms. This type of Tier 1 instruction lies at the heart of an RTI framework.

   Regarding subsequent tiers, this book explained the RTI framework in terms of three intervention tiers. However, Tier 2 interventions were described in terms of intensive and ultra-intensive interventions. Elsewhere this phenomenon has resulted in the framework being explained in terms of levels, rather than tiers, of instruction.

   Explaining the framework in terms of levels, as opposed to tiers, of instruction allows Level 1 to equate to Tier 1. However, Tier 2—as it is described in this book—is explained in a leveled framework in terms of multiple levels, such as Levels 2, 3, 4, and 5. Subsequently Tier 3, special education, is described as Level 6. Explaining the RTI framework in terms of levels flushes out the labor-intensive nature of the framework because one way that instruction becomes more intense at each level is to reduce the pupil:teacher ratio (e.g., from 5:1 progressively down to 2:1).

4. Labor costs for RTI-related implementation and oversight activities. These labor costs pertain to various RTI-related activities school personnel would perform as a part of their daily work scope. To accurately account for these costs personnel would have to meticulously document the time they spend engaged in each activity that is identified below.

   a. Professional development. Various professional development activities are involved with the framework. These include training staff, particularly new teachers, about (1) the design and implementation of a school's framework, (2) the elements that comprise what a school believes to be high-quality instruction and how its provision will be monitored, (3) the use of commercial materials, and, (d) new evidence-based practices.

b. Time spent in meetings. Numerous meetings will be held for the purposes of evaluating assessment data, discussing fidelity checks, developing Tier 2 interventions that go beyond any standard treatment protocol, and communicating with parents.

c. Fidelity checks. To realize the effectiveness of an evidence-based practice, those who use it must ensure that it is implemented as designed. This is referred to as fidelity of implementation.

A fidelity check is a protocol that is routinely employed for ensuring that an evidence-based practice has been implemented as designed. This check involves having one person conduct a structured observation of the individual who is implementing the evidence-based practice. A checklist that delineates the steps that comprise the practice is created, and the observer determines the percentage of the steps that the person who implements the practice demonstrates. In most cases at least 80 percent of the steps must be demonstrated for one to conclude that the practice is being implemented with fidelity.

d. Impromptu teacher conferences. Those who provide Tier 2 and Tier 3 services most likely will engage in impromptu, as well as formal, conferences with relevant school staff. These impromptu conferences may occur before or after school, or during the school day when students transition into and out of Tier 2 and Tier 3 services. During these short, informal conferences staff will share their thoughts regarding aspects of effective and ineffective instruction for certain students. While these conferences constitute a salary expenditure they can contribute to the provision of effective instruction.

e. Parent meetings. Staff will have to meet with students' parents, particularly the parents of students who receive Tier 2 and Tier 3 services, to discuss a student's lack of expected progress and the school's proposed action plans. The number of meetings that need to be held may be related to the relative complexity of an RTI framework's design. That is to say, it may be easier and less time consuming to explain a three tier framework than a six-level framework.

In addition to face-to-face meetings, routine protocols may be instituted to keep parents informed. The mode of communication that is used in these protocols can take many forms, ranging from daily notes to weekly phone calls to detailed mid-term progress reports.

In the long run these parent outreach efforts may prove to be very beneficial if they result in increased community support. This support may result from the community's acknowledgement of the sincere efforts school personnel are making on behalf of each student. This support may be translated into measurable and immeasurable contributions from the community, including citizens approving funding measures, such as the issuance of bonds, and volunteering their time to work on behalf of the school.

f. Program administration. A school administrator, or her designee, will have to spend time overseeing the entire implementation of the framework. A particularly time-consuming task will be creating and managing the implementation of a master schedule that ensures that each student is receiving appropriate instruction in his general education classroom while also receiving appropriate Tier 2 or Tier 3 services. Other time-consuming tasks might be conducting fidelity checks and conferencing with staff afterwards.

g. Misidentification costs. Regrettably school personnel are very familiar with the negative stigma that comes with identifying a student in need of special education services. This circumstance, in and of itself, is a strong argument in favor of any protocol that will reduce, or eliminate, the misidentification of students who need to be provided special education services. In terms of cost considerations, it is not possible to calculate the numerous associated costs which include (a) teachers' lowered expectations for student achievement and (b) students' lowered self-esteem and learned helplessness.

5. Opportunity costs. These costs pertain to students, staff, and the school community at large. While some of these costs can be quantified, others cannot.

Opportunity costs for students include educational opportunities they must forego in order to be able to receive Tier 2 or Tier 3 services. For instance, high school students may have to forego taking an elective or participating in a community service activity so that they can complete a class that provides them with needed Tier 2 services.

Teachers may have to forego attending a conference so that the money that would have been spent on this activity can be used to

provide Tier 2 services. Likewise, funding for amenities, such as ob
taining items for a science lab, may have to be re-appropriated to the
framework. Regarding opportunity costs that are related to the community, special events such as field days and holiday programs may
not take place because school staff must use their available time to
provide instruction rather than prepare for these activities.

If Not RTI. . .

The overarching practical consideration with respect to the cost of an RTI
framework is whether it is a conceptually sound approach to accounting for
the performance outcomes of every student. Any approach to school accountability that truly monitors the progress of each student will be costly. Thus,
one could argue that the framework should not be rejected based solely on its
total cost.

In fact, it is reasonable to assume that many would argue that accounting
for the performance outcomes of every student is appropriate considering the
long-terms costs to society that are realized when a student's poor school
performance results in his need for significant social safety net supports.
These costs are to be juxtaposed to the costs that would be incurred for the
school services that would result in this same student contributing to a local
tax base through productive employment.

Cost considerations for any approach to school accountability are a component of the "pay me now or pay me later" debate. In other words, arguments in favor of paying for an RTI framework to ensure each student's
attainment of valued, targeted, learning outcomes are justifiable when they
are compared to arguments in favor of less expensive approaches that result
in the need for a lifetime of social safety net supports. School personnel,
however, can contribute only so much to this debate. Many individuals who
are not involved in the day-to-day operation of public schools have much to
say in this discussion.

RESPONSE-TO-INTERVENTION AND HIGH SCHOOLS

The structure and operation of high schools often times differs markedly
from that of elementary and middle schools. Therefore, when the framework
is applied to high schools the framework's essential components may look
quite different from their implementation in elementary and middle schools.

This circumstance can be attributed to a number of factors. For instance,
whereas research has identified the content and instructional strategies that
comprise effective beginning reading instruction, there is much less guidance
concerning the components of high quality, effective instruction for teaching

subject matter content in algebra, biology, and history. Furthermore, there are not similar standardized formal screening and progress monitoring measures.

The discussion that is presented below highlights some of the ways that the essential components of a response-to-intervention framework are addressed by high schools. In particular, this discussion assumes that the framework is most likely applied to students who are in the ninth or tenth grade and whose performance is being monitored in reading, English/language arts, and mathematics.[11]

Screening

Both standardized and curriculum-based measures of academic achievement can be used to identify students who are either at risk for failure and may need to be provided Tier 2 or Tier 3 services, or who are functioning in a manner that necessitates the provision of these services. Additional measures that can be considered as students enter the ninth grade are their performances on state tests and the grades they have earned in relevant classes. Evidence of multiple class failures has been correlated with future class failures.

Progress Monitoring

Traditional measures of students' progress, such as grades on quizzes and tests, curriculum-based assessments, and final course grades can be used in a high school's response-to-intervention framework. These measures can be supplemented with data obtained from diagnostic measures, high stakes tests that are tied to graduation requirements, and related practice tests that are based upon the same state-standards as the high-stakes tests.

High-Quality Instruction and Evidence-Based Practices

As was noted above, scientific research that pertains to how to present high quality instruction in subject matter classes such as algebra, English, and biology, is not as extensive or well developed as is the research base for teaching students how to read, which is a major focus of instruction in elementary schools. Consequently, a starting point for presenting high quality instruction is ensuring that it is aligned with a state's standards (i.e., what gets taught is what gets learned). Additionally, universal effective teaching practices, such as the use of explicit instruction and scaffolding, need to be infused in the content area courses.

Tier 2

At the high school level these services consist primarily of remedial instruction that is designed to enable the student to earn a passing grade in a content area class and pass an associated high stakes test that is required for graduating with a standard diploma (if there is one). These services most likely will be presented to both large and small groups of students who are enrolled in a separate, complementary class for an entire semester, a co-lab class, or, perhaps, a seminar. Other existing resources, such as routinely scheduled study halls or after school teacher/peer led tutoring sessions, may also be designated as Tier 2 services.

Tier 3

As is the case in elementary schools, these services are likely to be presented in small group arrangements, but also may be provided in 1:1 instructional arrangements. While the services for students who are working to attain a standard diploma may directly supplement the content that is being taught in grade level, content area classes, more often than not these services will address basic academic skills students have yet to master (e.g., phonics, whole number operations, decoding).

Special Consideration: Self Advocacy

High school students can self-advocate for their Tier 2 or Tier 3 instructional needs. Student self-advocacy is not a central feature of elementary and middle school RTI frameworks.

RTI Services Align to School Needs

The specific needs that a high school's staff decides to address will dictate the services they will provide. Given the structure and mission of most high schools, more often than not the implementation of a framework will be used to increase the number of students who pass content area classes and related graduation tests. Another need that is addressed in the current era of school accountability is a school's dropout rate.

Tangential needs that pertain to both students' academic performances and graduation rates are improved literacy skills and daily attendance rates. While high schools may use a response-to-intervention framework to reduce the number of students who are referred for a special education eligibility determination, most high schools do not spend a relatively significant amount of time and effort addressing this need.

CHAPTER 7 COMPREHENSION CHECK

Now that you have finished reading the chapter, you should be able to:

- List three practical matters a school will need to address as it designs and implements an RTI framework.
- Discuss the issues a school will need to address as it implements an RTI framework's assessment component.
- Explain the meaning of both horizontal and vertical coordination in terms of proper school-wide supervision of the implementation of an RTI framework.
- List three professional development topics that pertain to the implementation of an RTI framework that a school might need to address.
- Identify one issue that a school needs to address when it implements an RTI framework.
- Discuss transparent and hidden expenditures that might be involved with the implementation of an RTI framework.
- Discuss two ways that the implementation of an RTI framework in middle and high schools may differ from its implementation in an elementary school.

NOTES

1. Jennifer Pierce and Dia Jackson, "Ten Steps to Make RTI Work in Your Schools. The 10," *Education Policy Center at American Institutes for Research* (2017).

2. Special Education Programs (US), *Essential Components of RTI: A Closer Look at Response-to-Intervention*, National Center on Response-to-Intervention, 2010.

3. Sarah V. Arden, Allison Gruner Gandhi, Rebecca Zumeta Edmonds, and Louis Danielson, "Toward More Effective Tiered Systems: Lessons from National Implementation Efforts," *Exceptional Children* 83, no. 3 (2017): 269–280.

4. Tam E. O'Shaughnessy, Kathleen L. Lane, Frank M. Gresham, and Margaret E. Beebe-Frankenberger, "Children Placed at Risk for Learning and Behavioral Difficulties: Implementing a School-Wide System of Early Identification and Intervention," *Remedial and Special Education* 24, no. 1 (2003): 27–35.

5. Brandi Simonsen, J. Freeman, S. Goodman, B. Mitchell, J. Swain-Bradway, B. Flannery, and B. Putman, "Supporting and Responding to Behavior: Evidence-Based Classroom Strategies for Teachers." *USA: US Office of Special Education Programs.* (2015).

6. Brandi Simonsen, George Sugai, and Madeline Negron, "Schoolwide Positive Behavior Supports: Primary Systems and Practices," *Teaching Exceptional Children* 40, no. 6 (2008): 32–40.

7. Douglas Fuchs and Lynn S. Fuchs, "Introduction to Response-to-intervention: What, Why, and How Valid is It?" *Reading Research Quarterly* 41, no. 1 (2006): 93–99.

8. Lynn S. Fuchs, Douglas Fuchs, and Donald L. Compton, "Rethinking Response-to-intervention at Middle and High School," *School Psychology Review* 39, no. 1 (2010): 22.

9. Mitchell L. Yell (2016). *The law and special education (4th edition).* Pearson.

10. Ibid.

11. National High School Center, *Tiered Interventions in High Schools: Using Preliminary" Lessons Learned" to Guide Ongoing Discussion* (ERIC Clearinghouse, 2010).

Epilogue

Every student's attainment of targeted learning outcomes is the centerpiece of the work that school personnel perform in the current era of school accountability. Consequently, there exists a need to establish a valid protocol that accounts for this centerpiece. A response-to-intervention framework is one such protocol.

In particular, since this protocol is predicated on how each student responds to interventions that are provided by school personnel, it is a valid approach. This approach collects and evaluates data pertaining to both students' attainment of targeted learning outcomes and school personnel's use of high quality, evidence-based interventions. Accordingly, the framework addresses the elements that comprise the foundation of effective school-based services for each student. Thus, this book has focused on explaining this valid protocol with the understanding that it, like every single other educational intervention, will need to be refined till it realizes its lofty expectations.

Glossary

Academic learning time. The amount of time that a student participates in instruction that is at his instructional level. Some educators have advocated that every minute of the typical 180 day school year should be considered to be academic learning time and, therefore, a strong justification needs to be made for using this time for any other purpose.

Accommodation. A change of the conditions under which a student is expected to perform an academic skill, rather than an alteration of the standard that has been set for the performance of the task (which is a modification). Accommodations may include, but are not necessarily limited to, the time that a student is given to complete a task, the manner in which the task is presented to the student, the mode of responding that is required from the student, and the arrangement of the setting in which the task is to be performed. The purpose for providing an accommodation is to ensure that a student's performance is a valid reflection of his ability to perform a targeted skill. Note that accommodations can apply to instruction and assessment.

Acquisition. The phase of learning during which a student attains knowledge or learns how to perform a skill.

Active student responding. Any overt display by a student of a behavior that indicates his response to a task directive that pertains to an assessment of the learning objective that is the focus of instruction. An example is when a student shows a "thumbs up" to indicate that he believes the correct answer is true in response to a true/false question that a teacher has posed to assess her students' acquisition of knowledge that pertains to her lesson's learning objective.

Allocated time. The portion of allotted time that is designated for specific instruction. During a seven and a half-hour school day, teachers may be required to teach language arts for ninety minutes. This length of time would be the allocated time for language arts instruction.

Allotted time. The time that is available for instruction. If a school is in session from 8 a.m.–3:30 p.m. then the school's allotted time would be seven and a half hours.

Anecdotal assessment. Anecdotal assessment essentially involves the telling of a story. An example would be when a teacher is encouraged to write a narrative in which they document the events they observed about a phenomenon of interest.

Assessment. Collection of data.

Attention directive. The behavior(s) a teacher exhibits for the purpose of communicating to students that they need to demonstrate behaviors that indicate they are attending to the teacher. An example of an attention cue would be a teacher snapping her fingers twice and then saying, "Eyes up."

Attention response. The behavior(s) a student exhibits, immediately following the presentation of an attention directive by the teacher, for the purpose of demonstrating that the student is attending to the teacher. An example of an attention response is the placement of the student's hands on his lap and feet flat on the floor while looking directly at the instructor and remaining quiet.

Behavior. A person's observable actions, which include anything a person says or does. (Also, see the definitions for the terms that apply to the various dimensions of behavior: frequency, duration, force, latency, locus, rate, and topography.)

Child-find. A requirement put forth in the Individuals with Disabilities Education Act that public schools must seek out children with disabilities who may qualify for the receipt of special education services.

Child with a disability. As defined in the Individuals with Disabilities Education Act, a child with a disability is a child who meets the eligibility criteria for one or more of the categories of disabilities that are listed and defined in the IDEA and, because of the disability, needs to receive special education services. In other words, the manifestation of the disability adversely affects the child's educational performance. This has been referred to as the two-part eligibility standard for special education services. Among other things, this definition means that a child may meet the criteria for having a disability but may not be functioning such that she needs to receive special education services (e.g., when the child's below average academic performance is not markedly different from that of her peers in the general education classroom, or when a child performs above average in spite of having a specific learning disability and neither the child nor his parents want special education services).

Class size. Refers to the total number of students in a class. Most often this term is associated with general education classrooms in which one teacher is assigned to teach the total number of students in the class.

Controlled variance. The systematic change of instructional conditions on a routine basis for the purpose of ensuring that a student can perform a behavior across people, settings, and conditions (i.e., the student can generalize a learned behavior).

Continuum of alternative placements. The various locations in which special education services can be provided to a child with a disability and which are delineated in the Individuals with *Disabilities Education Act* (IDEA). These placements include, but are not limited to, general education, resource, and self-contained classrooms.

Core curriculum. A listing of the knowledge and skills that teachers are expected to address in the instruction that they present and that students are expected to attain. The core curriculum is to be the focus of the instruction that is presented in general education classrooms. See also *General education curriculum.*

Criteria/Criterion. A standard against which a student's performance is judged (e.g., correctly reading nine of ten consonant-vowel-consonant words).

Criterion-referenced assessment. A criterion-referenced assessment compares a student's performance to a predetermined performance level on a targeted learning outcome, such as whether a student is able to name all twenty-six lowercase letters of the alphabet.

Curriculum. A listing of the knowledge and skills teachers address in the instruction that they present and that students are expected to attain. This definition addresses the knowledge and skills teachers actually address in their instruction, which may differ from the content that comprises the core curriculum.

Curriculum-assessment alignment. The process of ensuring that the assessment items, whatever they are, are directly related to the content that is listed in a curriculum.

Data. Information. The types of data vary greatly and include everything from relatively subjective anecdotal reports to empirical, scientific measurements of more well-defined phenomena, such as red blood cell counts. Hence, data include both qualitative (i.e., descriptive) and quantitative (i.e., numerical) information.

Differentiated instruction. Varying the instruction that is presented in either a large or small group arrangement so that students' various learning needs are met. An example would be presenting instruction that focuses on teaching the majority of the students in a group how to read high frequency words but also includes teaching a smaller number of students in the group the names of some of the letters that are used to spell the words. Differentiated instruction may include focusing on the content that is presented as well as the feedback that is provided, plus the social skills that are being taught. See accommodations and modifications.

Discipline-specific effective teaching practices. Interventions—that are supported by multiple research studies that have documented their effectiveness—which address either the content that is central to mastery of an academic discipline (e.g., learning phonics skills during beginning reading instruction) or the instructional strategies that enable students to master this content.

Duration. The length of time a student engages in a behavior.

Dysteachia. A term that has been coined to refer to the fact that some students' lack of progress in the general education curriculum is due primarily to the fact that they have not received quality formal instruction rather than the presence of an innate disability.

Early intervention service. A service that is designed to address a student's lack of attainment of targeted learning outcomes at the earliest possible moment for the purpose of not only remediating the learning challenge but also enabling the student to continuously make adequate progress in his age- and grade-level core curriculum.

Educational intervention. An intervention that is designed to enable a student to acquire knowledge or perform a skill that is delineated in a learning objective.

Educational significance. Refers to how practical the application of the results of a scientific study are in the field of education, particularly a typical public-school setting. For example, the results of a study may indicate that an intervention that is provided to a student with autism using a 1:1 pupil to teacher ratio for eight hours per day, five days per week is much more effective than an intervention that is provided in a self-contained classroom a student attends for six and a half hours per day, five days per week, and where the pupil to teacher ratio is 3:1. The difference between the two outcomes may prove to be statistically significant, in terms of the first intervention resulting in better student outcomes than the second intervention, but the educational significance of the difference may be deemed to be minimal since most public schools do not have the resources to provide each student with autism the same intervention that was provided in the study that reported better outcomes.

Educator. A person, such as a principal or teacher, who is involved in planning, directing, or presenting instructional services.

Effective instruction. Instruction that results in a student demonstrating mastery of the targeted learning objective.

Efficient instruction. Effective instruction that, relative to one or more other means of presenting effective instruction, requires less time, money, material resources (e.g., instructional materials, furniture, classroom space, etc.), and/or effort.

Engaged time. The amount of time that a student attends to the instruction that is presented.

Evaluation. A characterization of data, or value judgement (e.g., when a multidisciplinary eligibility determination team concludes that the assessment data collected on behalf of a student meets the criteria for a specific learning disability. Likewise, when the materials that comprise a student's performance portfolio are reviewed and then assigned a rating of proficient as opposed to basic).

Evidence-based practice (EBP). Educational interventions that have been shown, through multiple research studies to be effective. The quality of the studies are documented through a process called an evidence-based review.

Explicit. Clearly stated, as opposed to implied or assumed.

Explicit instruction. A type of teacher-directed instruction that involves having the teacher select the learning objective and then design a structured lesson that, as is appropriate, is comprised of (a) direct explanation and modeling, (b) guided practice, (c) independent practice, (d) assessment, and (e) lesson review.

Feedback. Information a teacher presents to a student and that either follows (a) a student's response or (b) the amount of time that has been established for marking that the student exhibited no response. Types of feedback include reinforcement and error correction.

Fidelity check. A protocol for ensuring that an evidence-based practice has been implemented as designed. It involves having one person conduct a structured observation of the individual who is implementing the evidence-based practice. A checklist that delineates the steps that comprise the practice is created, and the observer determines the percentage of the steps that the person who implements the practice demonstrates. In most cases at least 80 percent of the steps must be demonstrated for one to conclude that the practice is being implemented with fidelity.

Fidelity of implementation. The implementation of an evidence-practice as it has been designed.

Fluency. The rate of the performance of a behavior, expressed as amount per unit of time. Most often measures of frequency are expressed as amounts per minute (e.g., number of words typed or read per minute).

Force. The strength of a behavior (e.g., a student broke two pencils in half; the student's yelling could be heard as far as three rooms away from his classroom).

Formal assessment. A prescribed way of finding out what a student has learned, or how much she has improved during an instructional period. These assessments have standardized methods of administration and grading.

Formative assessment. Refers to when, meaning how often, an assessment is administered. Formative assessments are administered quite often (e.g., daily, twice per week). Some remember the meaning of formative assessment by associating the "f" in the word formative with the "f" in the word frequent.

Frequency. The number of times a student engages in a behavior; a count of the occurrences of a behavior.

Functional curriculum. A curriculum that is comprised of knowledge and skills that enable an individual to maintain himself as independently as possible in an age-appropriate environment. The content that comprises this curriculum are often referred to as activities of daily living or life skills. Examples of the knowledge and skills in a functional curriculum for an adolescent or young adult would include (a) learning to read the word "Exit" and that one of its meanings is to "Go out" and (b) how to do a load of laundry, cook a meal, and mail a package. A functional curriculum is often referred to along with references to a traditional academic curriculum that is comprised of knowledge and skills from content areas that include mathematics, English, science, and history/social studies.

General education curriculum. The curriculum that has been established for students in general education classrooms, grades preschool to twelve, to master. See *Core curriculum.*

Generalization. Behaviors that are consistently performed across people, settings, and conditions. Generalization can be demonstrated at any time and not just after initial teaching has occurred. For example, controlled variance may be employed during the acquisition phase of learning as an instructional strategy for the purpose of systematically addressing the teaching of generalization.

General least restrictive environment requirement. A concept that is addressed in the Individuals with Disabilities Education Act (IDEA) and that refers to the access a child with a disability has to typical peers and the general education setting in which these peers are educated— as well as the core curriculum they are taught. Specifically, in accordance with this requirement, the general education classroom is regarded as the default placement for students with disabilities, and the core curriculum stipulates the knowledge and skills they should be taught.

Hidden costs. Expenditures that are not readily accounted for as obvious expenditures of funds on response-to-intervention activities because these expenditures may be overlooked as they are associated with activities that are considered to be tangential rather than central to the implementation of a response-to-intervention framework.

Hidden curriculum. Refers to knowledge and skills that students may acquire that are not expressly stated in a published curriculum.

High-quality instruction. In an RTI framework high-quality instruction depicts the instruction that is presented in a general education classroom. High-quality instruction is the basis for Tier 1 services in the framework and, therefore, serves as the reference point for the instruction that is presented in all of the other tiers that comprise the framework.

High stakes test. A test that involves the application of important consequences.

Individuals with Disabilities Education Improvement Act of 2004. The federal law that directs the provision of special education services to children with disabilities in the United States. More commonly referred to as the Individuals with Disabilities Education Act or the initials IDEA.

Instruction. The act of teaching (i.e., imparting knowledge or skills).

Informal assessment. Informal assessment refers to various ways of collecting data without the use of standardized, formal methods. Examples of these assessments are teacher observations, student's daily classwork, and pop quizzes.

Instructional crack. A term that has been used to refer to a situation in which a student who demonstrates below average intelligence and concomitant below average levels of academic achievement does not qualify for the receipt of special education services and, therefore, may not receive additional services beyond those that are provided in a general education classroom to all students.

Instructional level. A term that refers to where a student is performing with respect to a performance standard that has been established for a particular student's age and corresponding grade-level. For example, a student may be identified as a fourth grade student based on his age but is noted to be demonstrating a need to master curriculum content that has been established for a student who is in kindergarten, such as naming the lowercase letters of the alphabet. Consequently, in terms of this student's literacy knowledge his instructional level would be would be designated as kindergarten level skills.

Instructional materials. Both the tangible (e.g., counting blocks, pencil, paper) and intangible (e.g., software applications) items that are used when instruction is presented.

Instructional setting. The location where instruction is presented, as well as its configuration. Instructional settings may include global environments as well as sub-environments within the global environments. For instance, a school may be designated as the global environment and a classroom a sub-environment within it.

Instructional strategy. The planned actions a teacher executes for the purpose of presenting instruction that is designed to enable students to demonstrate mastery of targeted learning objectives.

Integrated Framework. One name for a type of multi-tier framework that consists of protocols for simultaneously and efficiently addressing students' mastery of academic content and school social behaviors.

Intensity of instruction. A feature of multi-tier RTI frameworks. A number of the frameworks are predicated on the provision of more "intense instruction" to students who have not attained age- and grade-appropriate curriculum content through the instruction that has been presented in their general education classroom and is designated as Tier 1 services. The purpose, therefore, of presenting more intense instruction would be to enable the students to remediate curriculum content they have not mastered. The concept of intensity of instruction refers to measurable dimensions or features of instruction that are correlated to relatively more individualized and prolonged student engagement during a lesson. Specifically, increases in the intensity of instruction are intended to change, in a substantive manner, how instruction is conducted with students who are not demonstrating mastery of age- or grade-level appropriate curricula such that they experience more engaged and academic learning time in a lesson that pertains to a targeted learning objective, and this increase in engaged and academic learning time results in mastery of the learning objective. Examples of the dimensions of instruction that can be manipulated for the purpose of increasing the intensity of instruction include:

1. The use of lower pupil to teacher ratios
2. The allowance of more opportunities for students to engage in active student responding
3. The provision of more frequent and specific feedback by the teacher
4. The allowance for more allocated, engaged, and academic learning time
5. Higher rates of instructional trials per session

Intensity of instruction must be validated/determined to be effective with respect to a student's mastery of learning objectives.

Intensive intervention. Strategically designed interventions that consist of a number of elements that allow for more individualized and prolonged student engagement relative to the type of engagement students can experience as a result of being provided high quality instruction in a general education classroom through what are referred to as Tier 1 services in an RTI framework.

Intervention. A change of the environment that is intended to increase a student's display of a desirable behavior or decrease a student's display of an inappropriate behavior. Examples include reconfiguring the assigned seating for a class so that a student who has been exhibiting a high rate of off-task behavior is seated in a spot that is not as close—as was the case previously—to a potentially distracting stimuli (e.g., having a student sit in a location that is further removed from the pencil sharpener, which is accessed frequently by many students in the classroom) and providing a student with feedback after every response rather than after she completes all twenty trials that are presented by the teacher.

Knowledge. Information.

Large group instruction: A group whose composition consists of a pupil:teacher ratio of 9:1 or higher. In most instances large group instruction refers to general education classes in which twenty to thirty or more students receive instruction from one teacher (i.e., a pupil:teacher ratio of 20–30+:1). Also referred to as a large group arrangement.

Latency. The amount of time that elapses between the presentation of a task directive, from a teacher to a student, and the moment the student begins to perform the task.

Learning. A relatively permanent change in behavior that is the result of experience.

Learning how to learn. The concept that a student becomes more efficient at learning by developing an understanding of how instruction is routinely presented. An example would be a student knowing that when new material is being presented the teacher will first model how to demonstrate acquisition of the knowledge or skill and then will support the student with prompts until the student demonstrates the criterion level performance.

Learning objective. A student-specific statement, written using terms that allow someone to observe and objectively measure a student's behavior, which describes the content from the curriculum that the student will acquire, the conditions under which the student will acquire the content, and the criteria for mastery.

Level of learning. To the extent that a curriculum is vertically or horizontally sequenced, the level of learning refers to an arrangement where the learning of certain skills is to precede the learning of others. In terms of grade levels, at the end of the school year when a fourth grade student shows, on an assessment, that he has mastered only first grade math skills, he would be said to be performing at a lower level than a classmate who has demonstrated mastery of the fourth grade math skills. In terms of prerequisite skills, a student who has not mastered repeated addition would be said to be performing at a lower level than a student who has mastered basic multiplication facts.

Locus. The location where a student engages in a behavior (e.g., in the cafeteria at school).

Maintenance. The performance of a skill, over time, in accordance with the criteria that were set for mastery of the skill during the acquisition phase of learning.

Master/Mastery. Performing a behavior that is defined in a learning objective such that the established criterion for correct responding is met (e.g., reading ten high frequency words within thirty seconds across three consecutive assessment sessions); Perform the skill with accuracy, fluency, maintenance, and generalization in accordance with prescribed standards.

Meaningful education benefit. An ill-defined concept that refers to a student mastering the content in her curriculum such that the student's level of achievement during the period of instruction in question would be judged to be more than trivial progress but not necessarily indicative of the student's potential for maximum achievement.

Mode of responding. The behavior(s) a student exhibits when he emits a response. Examples include the use of speech, written responses, pointing, properly using a computer's interface (e.g., clicking on an icon on a screen), and the successful performance a skill, such as independently toileting oneself.

Modification. With respect to a child with a disability, a learning objective that is markedly different with respect to the age- and grade-appropriate curriculum standards that have been established for the student.

Multi-Tier System of Support (MTSS). Some form of a multi-tier intervention framework that is being employed by a school but is not being identified as an RTI framework, SWPBIS framework, or some form of an integrated multi-tier framework.

Norm-referenced assessment. A norm-referenced assessment compares a student's assessment results to an appropriate target group (e.g., other students the same grade), such as whether a student's score met or exceeded the scores of 75 percent or more of the students in his grade.

Operational definition. An explicit definition of the behavior a student exhibits such that two or more independent observers are able to agree upon its display by the student.

Opportunity cost. The identification of an activity that could not, or was not, performed because another matter was addressed. An example of an opportunity cost would be a student not receiving remedial, small group instruction because he was assisting others in putting students' school pictures in envelopes.

Overt behavior. A person's observable actions; anything a person says or does.

Pace of instruction. The rate at which instruction is presented (see definition for rate). For instance, pace could refer to the number of task directives, demonstrations, or topics presented during a unit of time.

Pre-referral to placement process. A protocol schools follow to identify children with disabilities. It is one part of the IDEA's mandatory effort, called Child Find, to locate every child who needs to receive special education services. A pre-referral to placement process consists of multiple elements that include identifying children who are demonstrating low academic achievement and then providing remedial instruction to ameliorate the student's low performance.

Problem-solving protocol. One approach to the provision of Tier 2 services that consists of a school-based team of professionals who work through a multi-step process on behalf of each student who exhibits an academic deficit or is not engaging in appropriate school social behavior. This process begins with the identification of the student's academic achievement or school social behavior deficit followed by an examination of various aspects of the deficit (e.g., what is the extent of the deficit, which interventions have already been used to address it, etc.). An individualized intervention plan is then designed and implemented, and student performance data are routinely collected and evaluated to determine the plan's effectiveness.

Progress monitoring. With respect to an RTI framework, refers to assessments that identify the level at which a student is performing as well as the rate at which the student learns new material.

Pupil:Teacher ratio. The number of students per teacher, or instructor, in an instructional setting. For example, 2:1 refers to two students with one teacher while 8:1 refers to eight students with one teacher. In a self-contained classroom in which nine students receive instruction from a teacher and two instructional assistants, the pupil to teacher ratio would be 9:3, which is the same as 3:1.

Prompt. Additional information that is provided by the teacher to the student after the task directive is presented. The primary purpose of the prompt is to increase the probability of that a student would emit a correct response that would be reinforced by the teacher. For instance, after a teacher showed the student an index card on which is written the word "cat" and presenting the task directive, "Read this word," the teacher would provide a prompt by saying the first two sounds that comprise the spoken form of the word.

Qualitative. Describing the quality of something in terms of size, appearance, value, and so on. This type of information gathering tends to be more subjective in nature.

Quantitative. Describing something that can be counted or measured in discrete units. This type of information can be used in statistical analysis.

Rate. A ratio of the frequency of a student's behavior per unit of time. Usually reported as a ratio of the frequency of a behavior per one minute (e.g., answering 6 basic additions fact correctly in one minute).

Rate of learning. Refers to the ratio of the number of new skills learned per unit of time. For example, if twelve new skills were learned in six weeks then the rate of learning would be two skills per week (12 skills:6 weeks is 2 skills:1 week).

Remediate. The correction of a deficiency. With respect to learning, remediation involves teaching a student content from the student's curriculum that she should have learned at specified performance level (i.e., criterion) at a previous point in time with respect to the scope and sequence of the curriculum.

Resource room. A classroom within a school in which children with disabilities receive instruction from 20 to 59 percent of the school day, inclusive.

Response-to-intervention framework (RTI framework). A multi-tiered, data-based protocol that focuses on how the core curriculum is taught in a general education classroom as well as elsewhere to students who have demonstrated a noteworthy lack of progress in mastering that curriculum.

School reform. One definition for the word reform is to improve upon the way that something is currently being done. Hence school reform refers to exploring ways that more effective, efficient instruction can be presented to students in public schools.

School social behavior. Behaviors that are appropriate in a particular school context (i.e., while on school premises or in an extension of these premises, such as a school bus). For the purposes of this book social behaviors are those that allow someone to share space appropriately with others.

School-Wide Positive Behavior Interventions and Support (SWPBIS). The name of a multi-tier framework that focuses on teaching students how to engage in appropriate school social behaviors.

Scientifically based instruction. Refers to the use of research to validate effective interventions. Constant time delay is an example of a scientifically based instructional strategy for teaching students with disabilities to read high frequency words.

Scope and sequence. The total number of skills delineated in a curriculum and the suggested order in which they are to be taught; All of the skills that comprise the student's curriculum (i.e., the scope) and the suggested order in which the skills are to be taught (i.e., the sequence).

Screen. To identify the smaller number of students, from among a relatively larger group, who need to be examined in more detail for some previously identified purpose, such as making better progress in the general education curriculum or the possibility of manifesting a disability that will result in the provision of special education services.

Screener. In an RTI framework, the purpose of a screener is to predict which students will not achieve expected learning outcomes if they continue in their current Tier 1 program, such as mastering end-of-the year benchmarks in reading and math. It is a type of assessment characterized by quick, low cost, repeatable testing of age-appropriate skills (e.g., identifying letters of the alphabet or reading a list of high-frequency words) or school social behaviors (e.g., tardiness, aggression, or hyperactivity). In the framework, screening is to be conducted two to three times per year.

Self-contained classroom. A classroom within a school in which children with disabilities receive instruction for more than 60 percent of the school day.

Session. The time during which small group instruction is presented.

Skill. The ability to perform a task, which is a piece of work.

Small group instruction. An instructional arrangement that consists of two to eight students, and 1 or more instructors such that the pupil to teacher ratio is not less than 2:1. Also referred to as small group arrangement.

Small group instructional arrangement. The location, as well as its set up, in which instruction is provided to a group of two to eight students and whose pupil:teacher ratio is at least 2:1 (as opposed to 1:1).

Social behavior. A behavior that involves engagement with at least one other human being.

Specially-designed instruction. A term that is defined in the Individuals with Disabilities Education Act and refers to the special education services that are to be designed and provided to a child with a disability. Specifically, the term refers to the content, methodology, or delivery of instruction.

Special education. Per the IDEA, special education is defined as specially designed instruction to meet the unique needs of a child with a disability.

Standardized assessment. An assessment that is conducted in a prescribed manner each time it is completed.

Standard treatment protocol. One approach to the provision of Tier 2 services that involves the use of a pre-packaged, research-validated intervention that has been designed to address a specific academic or school social behavior deficit (e.g., phonics skills, asking appropriate questions in class). This means that the instructor presents this intervention to every student in the small group "as it has been designed."

"Students who fall through the instructional crack." A phrase that refers to students who present below average scores on measures of intelligence and academic achievement, but not in a way that qualifies them for the receipt of special education services on the basis of being a child with a disability, such as a specific learning disability or intellectual disability. Rather, absent the use of an intervention process similar to the one put forth in a response-to-intervention model, these students would be expected to demonstrate mastery of grade-level standards in the general education curriculum with the receipt of only those services that are provided in the general education classroom via large group instruction.

Summative assessment. Summative assessments are administered periodically, most often following weeks of instruction. In most instances the goal of a summative assessment is to evaluate student learning at the end of an instructional unit by comparing the student's performance against some standard or benchmark (i.e. curriculum objectives, learning outcomes, district grading scales) as well as a unit pre-test.

Supplementary aids, services, and supports. Various forms/types of additional assistance that are provided on behalf of a child with a disability to enable him to receive appropriate special education services in a general education classroom or setting with typical, non-disabled peers.

Systematic. Clearly defined teaching procedures that can be readily replicated by others.

Targeted. That which is focused upon.

Targeted learning outcomes. Curriculum content that is identified in a learning objective and is the focus of the instruction that is presented to students.

Task directive. The directions a student is to follow for the purpose of emitting what is deemed to be a contextually correct response and, therefore, a demonstration that the student has mastered a learning objective (e.g., pointing to the letter "a" when it is presented on an index card along with four other lowercase letters of the alphabet; completing a load of laundry after reading the words, "Do Laundry," that are written on an individual's list of chores).

Teacher. An individual who, after completing an approved preparation program, has been awarded a license from a designated state agency that permits the person to be employed as a teacher in a state-approved educational agency such as a public school.

Teacher-directed instruction. An instructional protocol in which the teacher decides what will be taught, how it will be taught, how the student is to perform a skill, and when the student has mastered it. To teach the skill the teacher uses one of four basic instructional strategies—either individually or in combination—to demonstrate how the skill is to be performed and then directs with student to do it while providing appropriate prompts until the student is able to perform the skill independently in response to a task directive. Teacher-directed instruction also involves the provision of feedback by the teacher to a student after a student response or no response.

Teaching. Imparting knowledge or skills.

Teaching assistant. A person who is not a licensed teacher but does perform various tasks that assist in the provision of educational services to students. Synonymous titles include instructional assistant, teacher's aide, and paraprofessional.

Test, Testing. A condition under which a student is required to respond to a task directive. Testing can involve both independent and prompted student responses to a task directive, which can be written or oral.

Tiered intervention component. A classification system that is used to match students to the intervention services they require to address their learning needs.

Tier 1. In a response--to-intervention framework Tier 1 refers to high quality instruction that is presented in a general education classroom. In this book high quality instruction includes the use of evidence-based practices, which is another feature of Tier 1 instruction. Altogether this instruction is projected to be effective with 75–80 percent of the students.

Tier 2. In a response-to-intervention framework Tier 2 refers to services that are provided to the 20–25 percent of students who did not master targeted learning outcomes after receiving Tier 1 instruction. Tier 2 services also might be presented to students whose performance on a screener indicates that they most likely will need to receive instruction that supplements the instruction that is provided in Tier 1. Tier 2 services are characterized by the use of small group arrangements and the provision of more intense intervention than was provided in Tier 1.

Tier 3. In this book, Tier 3 services in a response-to-intervention framework consists of special education services.

Trial. Refers to an instructional sequence that consists of the presentation of a task directive by the teacher followed by an allowance for a student response (to include a no response option), the provision of feedback from the teacher, and an inter-trial interval.

Topography. The location on one's body where a student's behavior is exhibited (e.g., a student slaps the top of his right thigh with an open right hand).

Universal effective teaching practices. Universal effective teaching practices mostly refer to behaviors a teacher exhibits during a lesson and are appropriate for use irrespective of the academic subject matter or school social behaviors that are the focus of instruction. Examples of these practices include clearly stating the person's learning objectives, presenting material in appropriate chunks, frequently soliciting active student responding, and conducting a review at the end of a lesson.

Validity. Refers to whether a test measures the skill (or some other construct) that it purports to measure. For instance, a test which has been constructed to measures a student's math calculation and reasoning skills via the presentation of numerous word problems that a student needs to read independently may end up being more of a measure of a student's reading ability than math ability.

Bibliography

Abbott, Mary, Cheryl Walton, and Charles R. Greenwood. "Phonemic Awareness in Kindergarten and First Grade." *Teaching Exceptional Children* 34, no. 4 (2001): 20–26.

Abbott, Mary, Cheryl Walton, Yolanda Tapia, and Charles R. Greenwood. "Research to Practice: A 'Blueprint' for Closing the Gap in Local Schools." *Exceptional Children* 83 (1999): 339–362.

Adams, Marilyn J., "Beginning to Read: Learning and Thinking About Print." Cambridge, MA: MIT Press, 1990.

Algozzine, Bob, R. Putnam, and R. H. Horner. "Support for Teaching Students with Learning Disabilities Academic Skills and Social Behaviors within a Response-to-Intervention Model: Why It Doesn't Matter What Comes First." *Insights on Learning Disabilities* 9, no. 1 (2012): 7–36.

Algozzine, Bob, Chuang Wang, Richard White, Nancy Cooke, Mary Beth Marr, Kate Algozzine, Shawnna S. Help, and Grace Zamora Duran. "Effects of Multi-Tier Academic and Behavior Instruction on Difficult-to-Teach Students." *Exceptional Children* 79, no. 1 (2012): 45–64.

Anderegg, M. L., and Glenn A. Vergason. "An Analysis of One of the Cornerstones of the Regular Education Initiative." *Focus on Exceptional Children* 20, no. 8 (1988): 1–7.

Arden, Sarah V., Allison Gruner Gandhi, Rebecca Zumeta Edmonds, and Louis Danielson. "Toward More Effective Tiered Systems: Lessons from National Implementation Efforts." *Exceptional Children* 83, no. 3 (2017): 269–280.

Balu, Rekha, Pei Zhu, Fred Doolittle, Ellen Schiller, Joseph Jenkins, and Russell Gersten. "Evaluation of Response-to-intervention Practices for Elementary School Reading. NCEE 2016-4000." *National Center for Education Evaluation and Regional Assistance* (2015).

Barnes, Aaron C., and Jason E. Harlacher. "Clearing the Confusion: Response-to-Intervention as a Set of Principles." *Education and Treatment of Children* 31, no. 3 (2008): 417–431.

Brophy, Jere E. *Teaching.* International Academy of Education and the International Bureau of Education, 1999. Available at www.cklavya.org/edu-practices_01_eng.pdf.

Brophy, Jere. "Teacher Influences on Student Achievement." *American Psychologist* 41, no. 10 (1986): 1069–1077. Available at http://dx.doi.org/10.1037/0003-066X.41.10.1069.

Byrne, Brian, and Ruth Fielding-Barnsley. "Evaluation of a Program to Teach Phonemic Awareness to Young Children: A 1-Year Follow-Up." *Journal of Educational Psychology* 85, no. 1 (1993): 104–111.

Chaparro Erin A., Kathleen Ryan Jackson, Scott K. Baker, and Keith Smolkowski. "Effective Behavioural and Instructional Support Systems: An Integrated Approach to Behaviour and Academic Support at the District Level." *Advances in School Mental Health Promotion* 5, no. 3 (2012): 161–176. doi: 10.1080/1754730X.2012.707424

Chard, David J., and Edward J. Kameenui. "Struggling First-Grade Readers: The Frequency and Progress of their Reading." *The Journal of Special Education* 34, no. 1 (2000): 28–38.

Collins, Belva C., David L. Gast, Melinda J. Ault, and Mark Wolery. "Small Group Instruction: Guidelines for Teachers of Students with Moderate to Severe Handicaps." *Education & Training in Mental Retardation* 26, no. 1 (1991): 1–18.

Cook, Bryan, Virginia Buysse, Janette Klingner, Tim Landrum, Robin McWilliam, Melody Tankersley, and Dave Test. "Council for Exceptional Children: Standards for Evidence-Based Practices in Special Education." *Teaching Exceptional Children* 46, no. 6 (2014): 206.

Cook, Bryan G., and Sara Cothren Cook. "Unraveling Evidence-Based Practices in Special Education." *The Journal of Special Education* 47, no. 2 (2013): 71–82.

Cook, Lysandra, Bryan G. Cook, Timothy J. Landrum, and Melody Tankersley. "Examining the Role of Group Experimental Research in Establishing Evidenced-Based Practices." *Intervention in School and Clinic* 44, no. 2 (2008): 76–82.

Cook, Bryan G., Timothy J. Landrum, Lysandra Cook, and Melody Tankersley. "Introduction to the Special Issue: Evidence-Based Practices in Special Education." *Intervention in School and Clinic* 44, no. 2 (2008): 67.

Cook, Bryan G., Melody Tankersley, Lysandra Cook, and Timothy J. Landrum. "Evidence-Based Practices in Special Education: Some Practical Considerations." *Intervention in School and Clinic* 44, no. 2 (2008): 69–75.

Cook, Bryan G., Melody Tankersley, and Sanna Harjusola-Webb. "Evidence-Based Special Education and Professional Wisdom: Putting It All Together." *Intervention in School and Clinic* 44, no. 2 (2008): 105–111.

Cook, Bryan G., Melody Tankersley, and Timothy J. Landrum. "Determining Evidence-Based Practices in Special Education." *Exceptional Children* 75, no. 3 (2009): 365–383.

Education for All Handicapped Children Act, Pub. L No. 94-142. (1975).

Ehri, Linnea C. "Development of the Ability to Read Words." *Handbook of Reading Research* 2 (1991): 383–417.

Ehri, Linnea C., and Alison G. Soffer. "Graphophonemic Awareness: Development in Elementary Students." *Scientific Studies of Reading* 3, no. 1 (1999): 1–30.

Engelmann, Siegfried. "Theory of Mastery and Acceleration." *Issues in Educating Students with Disabilities* (1997): 117–195.

Epstein, Michael, Marc Atkins, Douglas Cullinan, Krista Kutash, and K. Weaver. "Reducing Behavior Problems in the Elementary School Classroom." *IES Practice Guide* 20, no. 8 (2008): 12–22.

Every Student Succeeds Act, Pub. L. No. 114-95, § 1, 129 Stat. 1802. (2015).

Felton, Rebecca H., and Pamela P. Pepper. "Early Identification and Intervention of Phonological Deficits in Kindergarten and Early Elementary Children at Risk for Reading Disability." *School Psychology Review* (1995).

Fletcher, Jack M., D. J. Francis, B. A. Shaywitz, B. R. Foorman, and S. E. Shaywitz. "Diagnostic Utility of Intelligence Testing and the Discrepancy Model for Children with Learning Disabilities: Historical Perspectives and Current Research." In *Workshop on IQ Testing and Educational Decision Making.* National Research Council, Washington, DC. 1995.

Fletcher, Jack M., Sally E. Shaywitz, Donald P. Shankweiler, Leonard Katz, Isabelle Y. Liberman, Karla K. Stuebing, David J. Francis, Anne E. Fowler, and Bennett A. Shaywitz. "Cognitive Profiles of Reading Disability: Comparisons of Discrepancy and Low Achievement Definitions." *Journal of Educational Psychology* 86, no. 1 (1994): 6.

Foorman, B. R., D. J. Francis, and J. M. Fletcher. "Growth of Phonological Processing Skill in Beginning Reading: The Lag versus Deficit Model Revisited." *Society for Research on Child Development,* Indianapolis, IN. (1995).

Foorman, Barbara R., David J. Francis, Jack M. Fletcher, Christopher Schatschneider, and Paras Mehta. "The Role of Instruction in Learning to Read: Preventing Reading Failure in At-Risk Children." *Journal of Educational Psychology* 90, no. 1 (1998): 37.

Fuchs, Douglas, and Lynn S. Fuchs. "Critique of the National Evaluation of Response-to-intervention: A Case for Simpler Frameworks." *Exceptional Children* 83, no. 3 (2017): 255–268.

Fuchs, Douglas, and Lynn S. Fuchs. "Introduction to Response-to-intervention: What, Why, and How Valid is It?." *Reading Research Quarterly* 41, no. 1 (2006): 93–99.

Fuchs, Douglas, Lynn S. Fuchs, and Donald L. Compton. "Smart RTI: A Next-Generation Approach to Multilevel Prevention." *Exceptional Children* 78, no. 3 (2012): 263–279.

Fuchs, Lynn S., Douglas Fuchs, and Donald L. Compton. "Rethinking Response-to-intervention at Middle and High School." *School Psychology Review* 39, no. 1 (2010): 22.

Fuchs, Lynn S., Douglas Fuchs, Allison Gandhi, and Rebecca Zumeta Edmonds. RTI Hits Adolescence—Will It Make It to Adulthood? A Case for Cautious Optimism. Center on Response-to-intervention. American Institutes for Research. 2016. Available at https://rti4success.org/sites/default/files/RTIAdolescence.pdf.

Gersten, Russell, Sybilla Beckmann, Benjamin Clarke, Anne Foegen, Laurel Marsh, Jon R. Star, and Bradley Witzel. "Assisting Students Struggling with Mathematics: Response-to-intervention (RTI) for Elementary and Middle Schools. NCEE 2009-4060." *What Works Clearinghouse* (2009). Available at http://ies.ed.gov/ncee/wwc/publications/practiceguides/.

Gersten, Russell, Douglas Carnine, and John Woodward. "Direct Instruction Research: The Third Decade." *Remedial and Special Education* 8, no. 6 (1987): 48–56.

Gersten, Russell, Donald Compton, Carol M. Connor, Joseph Dimino, Lana Santoro, Sylvia Linan-Thompson, and W. David Tilly. "Assisting Students Struggling with Reading: Response-to-intervention and Multi-Tier Intervention for Reading in the Primary Grades. A Practice Guide. (NCEE 2009-4045). Washington, DC: National Center for Education Evaluation and Regional Assistance, Institute of Education Sciences, US Department of Education." *National Center for Education Evaluation and Regional Assistance, Institute of Education Sciences.* (2008). Available at http://ies.ed.gov/ncee/wwc/publications/practiceguides.

Greenwood, Charles R., Barbara Terry, Carmen Arreaga-Mayer, and Rebecca Finney. "The Classwide Peer Tutoring Program: Implementation Factors Moderating Students' Achievement." *Journal of Applied Behavior Analysis* 25, no. 1 (1992): 101–116.

Hauerwas, Laura Boynton, Rachel Brown, and Amy N. Scott. "Specific Learning Disability and Response-to-intervention: State-Level Guidance." *Exceptional Children* 80, no. 1 (2013): 101–120.

Horner, R. H., G. Sugai, A. W. Todd, T. Lewis-Palmer, L. Bambara, and L. Kern. *Individualized Supports for Students with Problem Behaviors: Designing Positive Behavior Plans.* (2005).

Hudson, Tina M., and Robert G. McKenzie. "Evaluating the Use of RTI to Identify SLD: A Survey of State Policy, Procedures, Data Collection, and Administrator Perceptions." *Contemporary School Psychology* 20, no. 1 (2016): 31–45.

Individuals with Disabilities Education Act of 1975, 20 U. S. C. § 1400 et seq. (1975).

Individuals with Disabilities Education Improvement Act of 2004, 20 U. S. C. § 1400 et seq. (2004).

Juel, Connie. "Learning to Read and Write: A Longitudinal Study of 54 Children from First Through Fourth Grades." *Journal of Educational Psychology* 80, no. 4 (1988): 437.

Kamps, Debra M., and Charles R. Greenwood. "Formulating Secondary-Level Reading Interventions." *Journal of Learning Disabilities* 38, no. 6 (November/December 2005): 500–509.

Kamps, Debra M., Dale Walker, Erin P. Dugan, Betsy R. Leonard, Susan F. Thibadeau, Kathleen Marshall, Laurie Grossnickle, and Brenda Boland. "Small Group Instruction for School-Aged Students with Autism and Developmental Disabilities." *Focus on Autistic Behavior* 6, no. 4 (1991): 1–18.

Kern, Lee, and Nathan H. Clemens. "Antecedent Strategies to Promote Appropriate Classroom Behavior." *Psychology in the Schools* 44, no. 1 (2007): 65–75.

Lane, Kathleen Lynne, Erik W. Carter, Abbie Jenkins, Lauren Dwiggins, and Kathryn Germer. "Supporting Comprehensive, Integrated, Three-Tiered Models of Prevention in Schools: Administrators' Perspectives." *Journal of Positive Behavior Interventions* 17, no. 4 (2015): 209–222.

Maag, John W. *Behavior Management: From Theoretical Implications to Practical Applications*, 2nd edition. Belmont, CA: Edith Beard Brady. 2004.

McLeskey, James, Council for Exceptional Children, and Collaboration for Effective Educator Development, Accountability and Reform. *High-Leverage Practices in Special Education.* Arlington, VA: Council for Exceptional Children, 2017.

Mercer, Cecil D. and Ann R. Mercer. *Students with Learning Disabilities,* third edition. (Merrill, 1997).

Mellard, Daryl F., and Evelyn Johnson. *RTI: A Practitioner's Guide to Implementing Response-to-intervention.* Thousand Oaks, CA: Corwin Press. 2008.

Moats, Louisa Cook. *Speech to Print: Language Essentials for Teachers,* 2nd edition. Baltimore, MD: Paul H. Brooks Publishing Company. 2010.

Moats, Louisa Cook. "Teaching Reading Is Rocket Science: What Expert Teachers of Reading Should Know and Be Able To Do." Washington, DC: American Federation of Teachers. (Item no. 39-0372). (1999).

Moats, Louisa Cook, and Carol Tolman. *The Challenge of Learning to Read.* Sopris West Educational Services. 2nd Edition (2009): 57.

Morris, Robin D., Karla K. Stuebing, Jack M. Fletcher, Sally E. Shaywitz, G. Reid Lyon, Donald P. Shankweiler, Leonard Katz, David J. Francis, and Bennett A. Shaywitz. "Subtypes of Reading Disability: Variability Around a Phonological Core." *Journal of Educational Psychology* 90, no. 3 (1998): 347.

Morse, T. E. "Response-to-intervention and the Cost of Student Achievement." *School Business Affairs* 82, no. 8 (2016): 18–20.

National Autism Center. "Evidence-Based Practice and Autism in the Schools: A Guide to Providing Appropriate Interventions to Students with Autism Spectrum Disorders." (2009).

National Center on Intensive Intervention (NCII) at American Institutes for Research. *Data-Based Individualization: A Framework for Intensive Intervention.* ERIC Clearinghouse, 2013.

National Center on Response-to-intervention. RTI Implementer Series: Module 1: Screening—Training Manual. Washington, DC: U.S. Department of Education, Office of Special Education Programs, National Center on Response-to-intervention. (2012).

National Center on Response-to-intervention. RTI Implementer Series: Module 2: Progress Monitoring—Training Manual. Washington, DC: U.S. Department of Education, Office of Special Education Programs, National Center on Response-to-intervention. (2012).

National High School Center. *Tiered Interventions in High Schools: Using Preliminary" Lessons Learned" to Guide Ongoing Discussion.* ERIC Clearinghouse, 2010.

National Reading Panel (US), National Institute of Child Health, and Human Development (US). *Teaching Children to Read: An Evidence-Based Assessment of the Scientific Research Literature on Reading and Its Implications for Reading Instruction.* National Institute of Child Health and Human Development, National Institutes of Health, 2000. Available at http://www.nationalreadingpanel.org/Publications/summary.htm.

National Research Council. *Preventing Reading Difficulties in Young Children.* National Academies Press, 1998. Available at https://doi.org/10.17226/6023.

No Child Left Behind Act of 2001, PL 107-110, 115 Stat. 1425, 20 U.S.C. § 6301 et seq.

O'Connor, Rollanda E., Angela Notari-Syverson, and Patricia F. Vadasy. "Ladders to Literacy: The Effects of Teacher-Led Phonological Activities for Kindergarten Children With and Without Disabilities." *Exceptional Children* 63, no. 1 (1996): 117–130.

O'Shaughnessy, Tam E., Kathleen L. Lane, Frank M. Gresham, and Margaret E. Beebe-Frankenberger. "Children Placed at Risk for Learning and Behavioral Difficulties: Implementing a School-Wide System of Early Identification and Intervention." *Remedial and Special Education* 24, no. 1 (2003): 27–35.

Pierce, Jennifer, and Dia Jackson. "Ten Steps to Make RTI Work in Your Schools. The 10." *Education Policy Center at American Institutes for Research.* (2017).

Prince, Angela MT, Mitchell L. Yell, and Antonis Katsiyannis. "Endrew F. v. Douglas County School District (2017): The US Supreme Court and Special Education." *Intervention in School and Clinic* 53, no. 5 (2018): 321–324.

Rosenberg, Michael S., Lawrence J. O'Shea, and Dorothy J. O'Shea. *Student Teacher to Master Teacher: A Practical Guide for Educating Students with Special Needs.* Prentice Hall, 2001.

Sailor, Wayne. "Access to the General Curriculum: Systems Change or Tinker Some More?." *Research and Practice for Persons with Severe Disabilities* 34, no. 1 (2008): 249–257.

Sailor, Wayne. "Advances in Schoolwide Inclusive School Reform." *Remedial and Special Education* 36, no. 2 (2015): 94–99.

Shapiro, Edward S. "Tiered Instruction and Intervention in a Response to Intervention Model." *RTI Action Network* 381 (2014). Available at http://www.rtinetwork.org/essential/tieredin-struction/tiered-instruction-and-intervention-rti-model.

Shinn, Mark R., and Rachel Brown. "Much Ado About Little: The Dangers of Disseminating the RTI Outcome Study without Careful Analysis." (2016). Available at http://www.rtinet-work.org/images/content/blog/rtiblog/ shinn%20brown%20ies%20report%20 review.pdf

Simonsen, Brandi, Sarah Fairbanks, Amy Briesch, Diane Myers, and George Sugai. "Evidence-Based Practices in Classroom Management: Considerations for Research to Practice." *Education and Treatment of Children* (2008): 351–380.

Simonsen, Brandi, J. Freeman, S. Goodman, B. Mitchell, J. Swain-Bradway, B. Flannery, and B. Putman. "Supporting and Responding to Behavior: Evidence-Based Classroom Strategies for Teachers." *USA: US Office of Special Education Programs.* (2015).

Simonsen, Brandi, George Sugai, and Madeline Negron. "Schoolwide Positive Behavior Supports: Primary Systems and Practices." *Teaching Exceptional Children* 40, no. 6 (2008): 32–40.

Sparks, Sarah D. "Study: RTI Practice Falls Short of Promise." *Education Week* 35, no. 12 (2015): 1. Available at http://www.edweek.org/ew/articles/2015/11/11/study-rti-practice-falls-short-of-promise.html.

Special Education Programs (US). *Essential Components of RTI: A Closer Look at Response-to-intervention.* National Center on Response-to-intervention, 2010.

Stanovich, Keith E., and Linda S. Siegel. "Phenotypic Performance Profile of Children with Reading Disabilities: A Regression-Based Test of the Phonological-Core Variable-Difference Model." *Journal of Educational Psychology* 86, no. 1 (1994): 24.

Stanovich, Keith E. "The Sociopsychometrics of Learning Disabilities." *Journal of Learning Disabilities* 32, no. 4 (1999): 350–361.

Stecker, Pamela M., Douglas Fuchs, and Lynn S. Fuchs. "Progress Monitoring as Essential Practice Within Response-to-intervention." *Rural Special Education Quarterly* 27, no. 4 (2008): 10–17.

Stewart, Rachel M., Gregory J. Benner, Ronald C. Martella, and Nancy E. Marchand-Martella. "Three-Tier Models of Reading and Behavior: A Research Review." *Journal of Positive Behavior Interventions* 9, no. 4 (2007): 239–253.

Stewart, Rachel M., Ronald C. Martella, Nancy E. Marchand-Martella, and Gregory J. Benner. "Three-Tier Models of Reading and Behavior." *Journal of Early and Intensive Behavior Intervention* 2, no. 3 (2005): 115–124.

Strain, P. S., and G. Dunlap. "Recommended Practices: Being an Evidence-Based Practitioner." (2006): 2006. Available at http://challengingbehavior.fmhi.usf.edu/handouts/Practitioner.pdf.

Sugai, George, and Robert R. Horner. "A Promising Approach for Expanding and Sustaining School-Wide Positive Behavior Support." *School Psychology Review* 35, no. 2 (2006): 245.

Tankersley, Melody, Sanna Harjusola-Webb, and Timothy J. Landrum. "Using Single-Subject Research to Establish the Evidence Base of Special Education." *Intervention in School and Clinic* 44, no. 2 (2008): 83–90.

The Regular Education Initiative: A Statement by the Teacher Education Division, Council for Exceptional Children October 1986. *Journal of Learning Disabilities* 20, no. 5 (1987): 289–293. Available at https://doi.org/10.1177/002221948702000508.

Torgesen, Joseph K., Ann W. Alexander, Richard K. Wagner, Carol A. Rashotte, Kytja KS Voeller, and Tim Conway. "Intensive Remedial Instruction for Children with Severe Reading Disabilities: Immediate and Long-Term Outcomes from Two Instructional Approaches." *Journal of Learning Disabilities* 34, no. 1 (2001): 33–58.

Torgesen, Joseph K., S. Morgan, and C. Davis. "The Effects of Two Types of Phonological Awareness Training on Word Learning in Kindergarten Children." *Journal of Educational Psychology* 84, (1992): 364–370.

Torres, Caroline, Cynthia A. Farley, and Bryan G. Cook. "A Special Educator's Guide to Successfully Implementing Evidence-Based Practices." *Teaching Exceptional Children* 47, no. 2 (2014): 85–93.

Turnbull III, H. Rutherford, and Ann P. Turnbull. *Free Appropriate Public Education: The Law and Children with Disabilities.* Denver: Love Publishing Company, 1998.

U. S. Department of Education. "Supplementary Aids and Services." Center for Parent Information and Resources. Last modified November 2017. Available at https://www.parentcenterhub.org/iep-supplementary/.

Vaughn, Sharon, and Elizabeth A. Swanson. "Special Education Research Advances Knowledge in Education." *Exceptional Children* 82, no. 1 (2015): 11–24.

Vaughn, Sharon, Sylvia Linan-Thompson, and Peggy Hickman. "Response to Instruction as a Means of Identifying Students with Reading/Learning Disabilities." *Exceptional Children* 69, no. 4 (2003): 391–409.

Vellutino, Frank R., Donna M. Scanlon, Edward R. Sipay, Sheila G. Small, Alice Pratt, RuSan Chen, and Martha B. Denckla. "Cognitive Profiles of Difficult-to-Remediate and Readily Remediated Poor Readers: Early Intervention as a Vehicle for Distinguishing Between Cognitive and Experiential Deficits as Basic Causes of Specific Reading Disability." *Journal of Educational Psychology* 88, no. 4 (1996): 601.

Walker, H. M., E. Ramsey, and F. M. Gresham. "Antisocial Behavior in School: Evidence-Based Practices." Belmont, CA: Wadswoth/Thomson Learning. (2004).

Wolery, Mark, Melinda Jones Ault, and Patricia Munson Doyle. *Teaching Students with Moderate to Severe Disabilities: Use of Response Prompting Strategies.* Edited by Naomi Silverman. White Plains, NY: Longman Publishing Group. 1992.

Wong, Connie, Samuel L. Odom, Kara Hume, Ann W. Cox, Angel Fettig, Suzanne Kucharczyk, and T. R. Schultz. "Evidence-Based Practices for Children, Youth, and Young Adults with Autism Spectrum Disorder." *Chapel Hill: The University of North Carolina, Frank Porter Graham Child Development Institute, Autism Evidence-Based Practice Review Group.* (2014).

Yell, Mitchell L., *The Law and Special Education*, third edition. Edited by Jeffrey Johnston. New Jersey: Pearson Education, Inc. 2012.

Yell, Mitchell L., *The Law and Special Education*, fourth edition. Edited by Jeffery Johnston. New York: Pearson. 2016.

Yell, Mitchell L., and David F. Bateman. "Endrew F. v. Douglas County School District (2017) FAPE and the US Supreme Court." *TEACHING Exceptional Children* 50, no. 1 (2017): 7–15.

About the Author

Dr. Morse has worked in the field of education for nearly forty years, during which time he founded and directed a school for students with autism and held positions as a university professor, public school special education administrator, and special education teacher. He has authored nearly seventy articles in peer and non-peer reviewed journals and made numerous presentations at international, national, state, and local conferences. Presently he works as a behavior support specialist and instructional coach in a public school system in Louisiana. He continues to learn about the lifelong journey of individuals with disabilities from his interactions with several family members who received special education services while in school.